SUCCESSFUL DIETING TIPS

SUCCESSFUL DIETING TIPS

Compiled by Bruce Lansky

Meadowbrook Press

18318 Minnetonka Boulevard
Deephaven, Minnesota 55391

First printing August 1981
Third printing May 1982

Printed in the United States of America

Library of Congress Cataloging in Publication Data
Lansky, Bruce.
    Successful dieting tips.

    Includes index.
    1. Reducing diets. 2. Reducing—Psychological aspects.
3. Reducing diets—Recipes. I. Title.
RM222.2.L33   613.2'5   81-11028
ISBN 0-915658-43-7   AACR2
ISBN 0-915658-34-8 (pbk.)

ISBN (paperback): 0–915658–34–8
ISBN (hardcover): 0–915658–43–7
Copyright ᶜ 1981 by Bruce Lansky
Editor: Kathryn Ring
Asst. Editors: Joan Lake, Amy Rood
Designer: Terry Dugan
Production Manager: John Ware

CONTENTS

ACKNOWLEDGMENTS

Thanks to June Baker, Cathy Balogh, Louise Delagran, Beth Dooley, Cathy Fitzgerald, Carolyn Freese, Tom Grady, Kathe Grooms, Sharm Grooms, Ann Grummert, Jane Hertig (owner of Minnetonka Diet Center), Mary Johnson, Jean Lewis, Sue Ludwil, Ward Ring, Jan Schonwetter (executive director of the Upper Midwest division of Weight Watchers International) and Keith Sehnert, M.D.

The quotes from Dr. Barbara Edelstein on pp. 7, 29 and 52 are taken from *The Woman Doctor's Diet for Women* by Barbara Edelstein, M.D. Copyright © 1977 by Barbara Edelstein, M.D. Reprinted with permission of Prentice-Hall, Inc.

The quote from Jane Brody on p. 9 is taken from *Jane Brody's Nutrition Book* by Jane Brody. Reprinted with permission of W.W. Norton & Company.

The quote from Dr. Frank J. Bruno on p. 10 is taken from *Born to Be Slim* by Frank J. Bruno, Ph.D. Reprinted with permission of Harper & Row.

The quote from Meridee Merzer on p. 19 is taken from *Winning the Diet Wars* by Meridee Merzer. Reprinted with permission of Harcourt Brace Jovanovich, Inc.

The quotes from Dr. Jean Mayer on pp. 24 and 37 are taken from *A Diet for Living* by Dr. Jean Mayer, published by David McKay Company. Reprinted with permission.

The chart and the quote on p. 25 are taken from *The Complete Book of Running* by James F. Fixx. Copyright © 1977 by James F. Fixx. Reprinted with permission of Random House, Inc.

The quote from Dr. Richard B. Stuart on p. 36 is taken from *Act Thin, Stay Thin* by Dr. Richard B. Stuart. Reprinted with permission of W.W. Norton & Company, Inc.

The material marked by asterisks (*) on pp. 38 and 41 is from the 1980 Revised Edition of *Calorie Guide to Brand Names & Basic Foods* by Barbara Kraus. Copyright © 1971, 1973, 1975, 1976, 1977 by Barbara Kraus, 1978 by John R. Fernbach, Esq. and Murray Cohen, Co-Executors to the Estate of Barbara Kraus, 1979 by The New American Library, Inc. Reprinted by arrangement with The New American Library, Inc., New York, New York.

The quote from Dr. Joyce A. Bockar on p. 94 is taken from *The Last Best Diet Book* by Joyce A. Bockar, M.D. Copyright © 1980 by Joyce A. Bockar, M.D. Reprinted with permission of Stein and Day Publishers.

The quote from Dr. Frank Field on p. 96 is taken from *Take It Off with Frank* by Dr. Frank Field. Reprinted with permission of William Morrow & Company, Inc.

Preface

I was doing fine on a diet until I flew to New York on business. I didn't eat a thing until the stewardess offered me a bag of peanuts and a complimentary bottle of wine. Later, when she served dinner, I felt my diet was "blown" so I proceeded to eat the roll with all the butter, the salad with all the dressing, and every last drop and crumb of dessert.

The next day at a business lunch, I was back on my program ... until the waiter wheeled up the pastry tray. I hadn't eaten a nesselrode pie for years (for some reason I never see any in Minneapolis) and I decided to give it a try. By then, my diet really was "blown."

A neighbor of mine once shared her dieting woes with me. She had lost four pounds on the latest fad diet and was approaching her weight-loss goal ... until she baked a chocolate layer-cake for her son's birthday. A friend who's trying to lose weight told me how well he was doing on his diet ... until he went home for the holidays. An applicant for an editorial job came into my office for an interview. She mentioned that she had been dieting successfully ... until she lost her job and got depressed. She found herself at home, feeling unhappy, with nothing better to do than eat.

What are the special foods, situations or moods that have the power to knock you off your diet? If you think about these powerful "diet killers" for a moment, you'll realize that they'll always be a threat, no matter what diet you're on. How will starting a new diet help you when you're at a restaurant, a Super Bowl party, home for the holidays or feeling lonely ... any more than your old diet helped you in these situations?

What this book won't do is try to sell you a new diet. What it will do is help you recognize and overcome your "diet killers." We collected information from every possible source to find out what gave dieters the most trouble. Once we'd identified the most tantalizing temptations, we set out to discover how successful dieters had managed to resist them. We consulted with doctors, nutritionists, fitness experts, diet-group leaders, authors, actors, models, neighbors, workmates and friends to discover their secrets of success.

The tips we've collected will help you in every phase of dieting—from selecting a diet that's right for you to maintaining your weight loss. You already know how hard it is to lose weight and keep it off; the ideas in this book can help increase your odds of success.

Once you've read through the book, you'll see that it's organized for quick reference so that any time you've got a problem, you can easily find the appropriate page(s) of solutions. I expect I'll be referring back to this book, and adding to it, for as long as I'm watching my weight. I hope you do too.

And if you have some successful dieting tips that I've overlooked, please send them to me. When I've gathered a batch of terrific new tips, I'll revise the book and add them . . . along with acknowledgments for those who have contributed.

Chapter 1
BEFORE YOU BEGIN

Psyching Yourself Up

Once you've decided to start dieting, you won't want to wait too long to get started, but try to give yourself at least a week to get ready. Spend some time thinking about how you got overweight. By understanding your problem, you'll be best able to determine an appropriate dieting plan. Forget about miracles and realize that you'll be giving up INSTANT gratification in foods that make you gain weight for LONG-TERM gratification in being thin, in having a new body and a new life.

If you are to succeed, you'll need commitment to whatever diet you choose, confidence in yourself and patience to wait for results. Concentrate on these qualities and try to build them up in yourself. And, while you're not yet officially dieting, think of yourself as watching your intake. You may lose a pound or two before you actually begin—a psychological boost!

*Commitment—
confidence—
patience*

*I deserve better
for myself*

It's Time to Lose a Few Pounds When:

- You go out of your way to avoid looking in a full-length mirror.
- You never weigh yourself anymore; it's too depressing.
- You can't get into any of your clothes—except the ones you just bought.
- You're too embarrassed about your body to be as interested in sex as you once were.
- Your doctor says, "Lose 15 pounds, or go on medication."

It's Time to Lose a Lot When:

- Your stomach rests on your lap when you sit down.
- You have to shop in "large size" stores.
- Your friends say you have a "pretty face" or start calling you "jolly."
- You don't go to movies because the seats are too narrow.
- Your kids are ashamed to bring friends home.
- You avoid going out because of the way you look.
- Your doctor says, "Lose a lot, or your life's in danger."

Developing will power and order in your life

• **Resolve** not to believe the miracle claims of fad diets. Dieting is tough work; try to understand from the beginning that it will take a great deal of effort.

• **Create** some new goals and activities for yourself at home or work, in anticipation of substituting new enthusiasms for the old preoccupation with food.

• **Organize** your closets, clean your house, tend to your bookwork. A sense of order in one area of your life can serve as a model for other areas, and your meal planning and eating may fall into place more easily.

• **Experiment** to see how your hunger works: delay a meal by a few hours; skip a meal; don't eat at all for a whole day. Does hunger make you feel anxious, afraid or proud of yourself? Whatever the emotion is, remember that's what you'll be dealing with later.

• **Order** the diet plate when you eat at restaurants to see how others react—and how YOU react.

• **Redefine** hunger as GOOD, not BAD. Your body is burning up fat!

• **Visualize** "junk food" as BAD. Remember that junk foods are Continuously Advertised Nutritionally Deficient Yummies (as used in the title of Vicki Lansky's *The Taming of the C.A.N.D.Y. Monster*).

• **Avoid** talking about food, eating or dieting with family or friends, at least for a while. Save your thoughts and ideas to strengthen your will when you start dieting.

Positive imaging

• **Daydream.** Look into the future. Picture yourself as good-looking, slim, energetic and occupied in interesting pursuits.

• **Imagine** yourself looking great at the beach.

• **Find** an article of clothing that fit you well 10, 20 or 30 pounds ago—or buy something new in the size you want to be—and try working back into it.

• **Highlight** your own good features. For example, have your hair styled in a new way.

• **Picture** yourself doing well in a wonderful new job, one you wouldn't dare aspire to today because you're not slim enough.

• **Visualize** yourself on a scale, weighing in at your target weight.

Important steps to take

1. Have a medical checkup if you have a significant number of pounds to lose or if you have a serious medical problem. Ask your doctor for recommendations about dieting.

2. Buy a diet cookbook and start reading menus and recipes. Also look for diet recipes and menus in magazines and newspapers; clip these for your own files.

3. Assign yourself a daily dose of humor. Life's not all grim, even though you may not be eating all you want to.

4. But STOP being a "good sport" about being overweight; no more laughing at yourself about it!

I can do it!

Take a personal inventory

☐ **List** the reasons why you want to lose weight.

☐ **Record** some of your feelings about yourself as you are now. Draw a sketch of your body as you think it looks now and another of how you'd like it to look someday.

☐ **Use** your tape measure to record all your measurements in preparation for serious record keeping. (See p. 29.)

☐ **Concentrate** on self-esteem boosters: accomplishments you're proud of and personal qualities of yours that you like.

☐ **List** all the healthful low-calorie foods you really like.

☐ **Record** your eating patterns for a week. Write down what you ate, when, where and with whom you ate it, and what kind of mood you were in. Be honest—were you neutral, content, tense, depressed? Save the record; you'll want to continue keeping it and refer to it often during both your dieting and maintenance periods. (See p. 30.)

☐ **Recognize** your "enemy." Start to identify those influences or "triggers" that cause you to lose control of your eating—that drink before dinner, food commercials on TV, the constant teasing of a toddler, any stressful situation.

☐ **Decide** which foods and situations you can handle easily and which you'll have to concentrate on—knowing what you have to fight is half the battle.

☐ **List** dangerous foods and situations in the imperative: "I WILL NOT go to the kitchen when I see a food ad on TV." "I WILL NOT eat when the kids are teasing."

Preparing others

- Tell EVERYONE about your decision and get your friends and family on your side.

- Explain how important weight loss is to you; ask your friends and family for help. But do this only if you'll be able to accept their help without resentment.

- Suggest to family members that they read some of the better dieting articles and books that you've been collecting.

- Announce to your family that you, at least, will buy no more high-calorie snacks to stockpile at home. If they want such things, they'll have to buy them and eat them somewhere else.

- Ask everyone NOT to give you candy or any other food, if they really love you.

Dr. Barbara Edelstein,

author of *The Woman Doctor's Diet for Women*

"It takes a lot of psychic energy to stick out a diet, and the kind of dedication most women reserve for being a wife and mother. But if you never let your guard down, no matter what is going on around you, you will come through the experience a thinner person."

You're In Trouble If You:

- stockpile treats at home, in your car, in your desk at the office.
- eat faster than others at the table with you.
- believe you MUST clean your plate at every meal.
- feel a sweet dessert is a necessity after a big meal.
- snack off and on all day, wherever you are, instead of eating only at regular times.
- comfort yourself with food whenever you're angry, depressed, worried or bored — or reward yourself with food when things go well.

- eat unconsciously or absent-mindedly, when you're not really hungry.
- use "business" as an excuse to eat great big lunches.
- never skip the treats at the coffee break.
- follow one taste of something you like with a gluttonous binge, making yourself uncomfortably full.
- sample everything you're cooking.
- have a bite with each family member when mealtimes are irregular.
- finish all the leftovers and eat up the scraps on children's plates.

Deciding How You Will Diet

Whether you choose to join a diet group, set up your own informal group or go it alone, you'll want to find a diet that will produce weight loss and (unless you're very overweight and addicted to bad habits) that will require no drastic changes in your lifestyle. Of course some changes in habits and attitudes will be necessary—if they weren't, you wouldn't be thinking about dieting! Be prepared to use all available "tools": you might start out on your own, move into a diet group if dieting alone isn't working and later try a diet counselor. The most important step is to find the way that works best for you—and to be careful not to finally commit yourself to a plan you know you won't like and won't follow.

Diet Selection Checklist

Fasting or going on a fad diet for a few days probably won't hurt you if you're basically healthy, and a quick dramatic weight loss may give you a nice boost at the beginning of a diet program. However, if you're planning to stick to a diet for some time, be more cautious, both for the sake of your health and to improve your chances of success.

Your reducing diet should include:

☐ **Sound nutrition.** We need foods from all four food groups if we are to be healthy and fit. (See p. 36.)

☐ **Variety.** Your diet should allow you enough different foods within each of the four food groups to help you avoid boredom as well as to provide good nutrition.

☐ **Flexibility.** Your diet should be adaptable to your habits and tastes. With modifications for weight maintenance, it should be one you can live on for the rest of your life.

☐ **Promise of reasonable but not excessive weight loss.** Statistics show that those who keep unwanted weight off are those who lose it slowly and gradually, over a period of time.

☐ **Absence of fanciful statements and promises.** Be skeptical; don't be taken in by such ideas as "magic," "new discovery," "totally new concept," "easy" or "eat all you want."

☐ **Credibility.** The diet author or diet-group leader should have the proper credentials in nutrition and weight-loss techniques.

Dieting in a group

• **Analyze yourself.** Are you a do-it-yourself loner or a "groupie" who'll do best in the company of, and with the support of, others?

• **Talk with friends about their experiences** in diet groups. Read all the available books and articles about these groups.

• **Call diet groups and centers for information** about programs and costs. Attend a meeting or two of the groups that interest you; most allow a free trial visit or offer a meeting at reduced rates. You may also wish to get information about programs in local hospitals, health centers or behavior-modification clinics. Some who can afford them like to spend time regularly at reducing spas or deluxe diet clinics.

• **Consider costs if finances are a problem.** Some diet groups do not have membership fees; others are quite expensive.

Jane Brody,
author of *Jane Brody's Nutrition Book*

"Every fad diet is nutritionally unbalanced in one way or another, and some are downright dangerous ...."

It's Been Reported That ...

... Margaux Hemingway, who belongs to the you-can-never-be-too-thin-or-too-rich culture, says, "My whole life is a diet!"

Choose a diet you can live with

For Better or For Worse   **by Lynn Johnston**

Ground rules for diets for two

Do's

• **Pick your dieting companion carefully;** find someone with goals comparable to yours.

• **Plan to get together frequently with your companion** and to make good use of the "buddy system." You'll talk together about dieting techniques, goals and frustrations; encourage each other during hard times; and perhaps exercise together.

• **Keep records together,** using the same kinds of forms (see pp. 30 and 34).

• **Shop for groceries together** sometimes, to make the hard moments in the cookie aisle easier.

• **Plan to have the man in a dieting team** eat any extra calories he's allowed at meals or snacks the couple doesn't take together. She'll be spared temptation and resentment.

Don't's

• **Don't make bets about who will lose most, fastest,** unless you're sure that you won't cause guilt feelings and resentments.

• **Never use pounds as goals;** use percentages of starting weights if you DO make a contest of dieting.

• **Try not to police or nag each other;** you could break up a good relationship.

• **Don't forget that if partners are of opposite sexes,** the man will probably lose weight more rapidly than the woman. This is because his body composition contains proportionately more muscle and less fat than hers. Men can also trade calories—exercise for food—more easily than women can.

Dr. Frank J. Bruno,
author of *Born to Be Slim*

"I sometimes think that the greatest enemy of the overeater is inertia. Thinking about, talking about, and reading about losing weight are all great. But they aren't the same as *doing it*. No weight will be lost if you don't take action."

It's Been Reported That . . .

. . . Richard Dreyfuss, Farrah Fawcett, Ben Vereen, Barbra Streisand and Elizabeth Taylor visit luxurious reducing spas when they want to lose weight. And that Cheryl Ladd, Diana Ross, Dustin Hoffman and Henry Winkler frequent a restaurant that offers special diet foods and an exercise studio.

Dieting alone

• **Be aware that your commitment to dieting** must be VERY strong. Giving up will be easier for you than for members of a group because not many people will know or care if you quit.

• **Talk with people who have successfully dieted alone** and ask them for help.

• **Consider keeping your diet a secret**—think how nice it will be when someone comments on your loss of weight!

• **Remind yourself continually that YOU are in control** of your lifestyle and that you're capable of choosing your own food and deciding when and how you will eat it.

• **Find or make up a prayer for self-control** and say it to yourself often—morning, night and in between. It should include the statements that you love yourself, even though you may have lapsed, and that you want to take care of your body, eating healthful foods in moderation and completely avoiding "dangerous foods."

• **Be careful about keeping records** (see p. 29) and weighing yourself regularly. You won't have the positive example and support of dieting companions.

• **Praise yourself generously** each successfully completed day.

Marty Ingels

"My diet secret? SWEET SURRENDER! I am one of those unfortunately incurable 4 a.m. Twinkie-Sundae-Pizza-holics who has failed every diet test from Drinking Man's to Mayo, Scarsdale, Protein, Mega-Vitamin, Feingold, Hypno ... all the way to fridge locks and glaring full-length kitchen shots of Orson Welles and Shelley Winters. I have struggled with more grapefruits than Cesar Chavez, more 'substitute foods' than a Bangladesh supermarket. I have wired everything shut but my jaw and have only become the world's fastest wire cutter ... until now.

"I HAVE FOUND MY MOUNTAIN OF THIN (nothing else works). I HANG AROUND WITH FAT PEOPLE—obese if possible—the bigger and wider and rounder the better (my best friend is an ex-circus star). Suddenly, I don't look too bad, and I don't give up an available Twinkie. The only problem is that it has caused a definite threat to my marriage. Why? My wife's two best friends are Fred Astaire and Joey Heatherton!"

Make a commitment

Setting Realistic Goals

Be aware that your best weight is not necessarily ideal for anyone else. A combination of gender, height and body build can help to determine how much you should weigh.

Don't set a higher ideal weight than you should, but remember that metabolism differences and the weight at which you feel most comfortable should also be considered. If you belong to a diet group, the leader will help you set your weight-loss goal.

Your dieting timetable

• **Plan to lose weight gradually,** over a period of time, in order to avoid disappointment and to give your body ample time to adjust. Remember that your weight did not come overnight; it won't go away overnight, either.

• **Break your total loss into reasonable divisions,** depending upon how many pounds you have to lose. Consider aiming for a pound or two a week—or a five-to-ten-pound unit in so many weeks—or a 10 percent loss within a certain time. In most cases, it will be best to keep your immediate goal at less than 20 percent of your total weight.

• **Build in some time for plateaus and occasional lapses,** especially if you're scheduling rigidly. This helps you to avoid setting yourself up for a guilt trip.

• **Keep your long-range goal in mind,** and think about where you'd be today if you had started your diet a year ago!

Calorie Intake Leading to Weight Loss

The average adult American consumes about 3,200 calories per day.

3,500 calories equal one pound of fat for you.

500 less calories per day will give you a one-pound-per-week loss.

1,000 less calories per day will give you a two-pound-per-week loss.

(See calorie requirements for weight maintenance on p. 99.)

Deciding how much to lose

• **Think back to the days when you felt vital** and full of energy—at your very best. Your weight then might be a realistic goal today.

• **Look over the clothes you used to feel good in** and would like to wear again. Your weight when they fit might be best for you now.

• **Set your actual goal weight at from two to five pounds below your ideal weight** to give yourself a little leeway when you get to the maintenance stage.

Two Ways to Figure Your Ideal Weight

1. Measure your height without shoes. Take the number of inches over five feet and multiply it by five-and-a-half. To this number add 110. This will be your ideal weight, according to a book of folk medicine by D. C. Jarvis, M.D.; note that many people think it is too high.

2. Or if you're a woman, give yourself 100 pounds for five feet, and add five pounds for every inch over that height. If you're a man, give 106 pounds for five feet, and add six pounds for every extra inch of height.

"Don't laugh, they've helped me lose 9 ounces."

Desirable Weights for Men and Women
According to Height and Frame, Ages 25 and Over

HEIGHT (In Shoes)*	Weight in Pounds (in Indoor Clothing)		
	SMALL FRAME	MEDIUM FRAME	LARGE FRAME
MEN			
5' 2"	112-120	118-129	126-141
3"	115-123	121-133	129-144
4"	118-126	124-136	132-148
5"	121-129	127-139	135-152
6"	124-133	130-143	138-156
7"	128-137	134-147	142-161
8"	132-141	138-152	147-166
9"	136-145	142-156	151-170
10"	140-150	146-160	155-174
11"	144-154	150-165	159-179
6' 0"	148-158	154-170	164-184
1"	152-162	158-175	168-189
2"	156-167	162-180	173-194
3"	160-171	167-185	178-199
4"	164-175	172-190	182-204
WOMEN			
4'10"	92- 98	96-107	104-119
11"	94-101	98-110	106-122
5' 0"	96-104	101-113	109-125
1"	99-107	104-116	112-128
2"	102-110	107-119	115-131
3"	105-113	110-122	118-134
4"	108-116	113-126	121-138
5"	111-119	116-130	125-142
6"	114-123	120-135	129-146
7"	118-127	124-139	133-150
8"	122-131	128-143	137-154
9"	126-135	132-147	141-158
10"	130-140	136-151	145-163
11"	134-144	140-155	149-168
6' 0"	138-148	144-159	153-173

*1-inch heels for men and 2-inch heels for women.

Note: Prepared by the Metropolitan Life Insurance Company. Derived primarily from data of the Build and Blood Pressure Study, 1959, Society of Actuaries. Reprinted with permission of the Metropolitan Life Insurance Company.

Your scale will tell you how you're doing on your diet —if you consult it

W.E.I.G.H.T.: When extra inches go, how thrilling

Getting Your Home Ready

What does your home have to do with your weight? Plenty! Because it's the one place where you can relax and really let yourself go, it probably is also the place where many of those extra pounds were added. You'll want to think about making the spots where you read (and eat), watch tele-vision (and eat), do paper-work (and eat), and just sit around chatting (and eat-ing) "off limits" for food. From now on, meals and snacks will be eaten only at the kitchen or dining-room table. If you do the cooking (or help or watch the cook), you'll want some changes made in the kitchen.

Getting your kitchen in shape

• **Move supplies** for hobbies and book work to another room. And move the television set, too, if you have one there.

• **Put all sweet and salty snacks out of sight,** in the freezer or in hard-to-reach places; or get rid of them altogether!

• **Store utensils for fancy baking in the basement** or some other inconvenient place. You may want to keep bread-baking utensils handy—if you can't avoid the urge to bake someday, at least bread will be something you can eat.

• **Make room on the counter** for any appliances you have that will cut food preparation time and lessen your temptation to nibble—a blender, food proces-sor or counter-top broiler.

• **Get a 6-foot phone cord** to replace the 12-foot one, which allows you to roam around the kitchen to get food while you talk.

• **Store the most tempting foods in opaque containers** in the refrigerator—if you can't see the foods, you won't be as apt to eat them!

• **Put some brightly colored stickers on the drawers** in the refrigerator vegetable and fruit sections—that's where you'll be looking from now on!

• **Remove the light bulb from your refrigerator** so you won't see all the goodies so clearly.

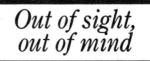

Out of sight, out of mind

Getting rid of high-calorie foods on hand

• **Give your remaining high-calorie foods** to your neighbors, your favorite charity or your worst enemy.

• **Throw them in the garbage!** That's better than becoming a human garbage pail.

• **Resist saving snack foods for "him," "her" or "the kids,"** if you can. What's bad for you is bad for them.

• **Use your cake or cookie mixes** to make treats for a scout troop, a nursing home or your slender friends at the office.

• **Prepare all the fattening foods you have on hand** and invite your friends to one last disgusting, farewell-to-fat party.

Kitchen Equipment That Will Help You Lose Weight

• **A steamer** to preserve nutrients and color in vegetables.
• **A centrifugal-spin dryer** to make your salad greens crisp and tasty.
• **Plastic containers** of various sizes to hold fresh raw vegetables and keep them crisp and crunchy.
• **Several sharp knives** for preparing vegetables, boning chicken and cutting fat from meats.
• **Non-stick pans** that eliminate the need for oil or grease.
• **A crock pot or slow cooker** to help you avoid watching (and sampling) cooking foods.
• **A pressure cooker** to speed up your cooking and get you out of the kitchen faster.

• **An egg coddler or poacher** so you won't be tempted to fry your eggs.
• **A wok pan** for quick food preparation and minimum calories.
• **A fat-skimming brush** for grease-free meat juices and soups.
• **A kitchen scale and measuring cups and spoons** to help you be sure you're eating recommended amounts of food.
• **A rack for your roaster** so grease will go to the bottom of the pan, instead of into the meat.
• **Several small pans** to encourage you to cook small portions.
• **A popcorn maker** that uses only air, requiring no oil.
• **A kitchen timer** with a loud ring, so you won't have to hang around the kitchen waiting for things to get done—or a portable timer that you can carry with you anywhere in the house.

Outfitting the bathroom

• **Position your easy-to-read bathroom scale on a level surface** so that it will register your weight consistently. Consider buying an accurate stand-up scale—the kind your doctor has in his office.

• **Get a good tape measure** to keep in your bathroom cabinet so it will be convenient for you to keep track of your losses in inches.

• **Treat yourself to new skin-care products** and fluffy towels or bath sheets to make caring for your body a pleasure.

• **Put a radio in your bathroom** to help make the room comfortable and cheerful.

• **Enjoy the time you spend in your bathroom!** Try to make yourself think of your bathroom, rather than your kitchen, as the "comfort zone" in the house.

Kitchen Reminders

☐ Put a self-stick mirror tile or two on your refrigerator door so you'll see your "compulsive eating" look (and notice that your face is already too fat).

☐ Attach a bell to the refrigerator door or to the door of the cupboard where snacks are stored. When the bell rings, shut the door! Or get a "Diet Conscience," a battery-operated unit that speaks to you with diet reminders when the door is opened.

☐ Tape on your refrigerator door, or attach with magnets, a calorie list, a few diet cartoons and some peppy one-line reminders.

☐ Put a scale in front of the refrigerator where you'll step on it before you give in to cravings.

Bathroom Reminders

☐ Hang a full-length mirror opposite the tub or shower, where you'll have to see yourself often and will be reminded to stick to your diet.

☐ Tape the best photo you have of your slender self to the mirror as a reminder of how you want to look.

Charles Wetherall,
author of *Quit* and *Diet*
"When I get two pounds overweight and I know I've got to get my diet in action, I go to the bathroom and look into the mirror and pledge, out loud, that I will stick to my diet."

For inspiration and better understanding

• **Take a look at any photos you can find that show a skinnier you.** Keep your high-school annual, college yearbook or wedding album (whichever your best self appears in) handy for inspiration.

• **Hang your favorite outgrown outfit** at the front of your closet, where you can see it often and be reminded of your goal.

• **Read the kind of self-help books that appeal to you most** — autobiographical, religious, behavior modification, exercise.

Your mind controls your body as a rider controls a horse

• **Learn about nutrition** so that you can better understand the principles of diet and the foods you should eat. Keep the information close at hand for easy referral.

• **Write yourself a serious letter** about why you are tired of being overweight. You'll want to reread it later, in weak moments.

I can't = I've decided not to

Final Plans for Starting Your Diet

Plan to start dieting on the day that's the very best for you, but don't put it off for too long. Try to be rested so that you'll feel calm and relaxed. Some women don't like to start dieting during the pre-menstrual days or the early days of a period. Others deliberately choose those days because their hunger lessens then and they'll have a water loss—a morale-lifting weight loss at the end of a period. Don't double the challenge of dieting by quitting smoking or giving up coffee, at least during the first weeks of your diet. And don't let yourself indulge in one last binge the day before you start!

The best day to start

• Check your calendar for a slow social period—a time when you can avoid eating in restaurants.

• Choose a meaningful anniversary, such as your birthday, or a "first," such as the first of the year, month or week. Or start at the change of seasons or a change in your own living situation, to make the beginning date of your diet important and easy to remember.

• Find a time when you'll be too busy with work or a project to think much about food.

• Look for a season when you'll be able to indulge in one or two of your favorite sports, or perhaps take up a new one that appeals to you.

• Pick a time when at least some of your favorite fruits and vegetables are in season (or available at reasonable prices).

Be the boss of what goes in your mouth

Meridee Merzer,
author of *Winning the Diet Wars*
   "To succeed permanently at weight loss and weight maintenance, some changes must be made in your lifestyle. You must find other things to do besides eat to reward, comfort and console yourself."

First days' checklist

☐ Plan to spend as much time as possible with friends who have successfully lost weight—they'll be your best inspiration.

☐ Make dates to go places where you won't be tempted to eat or to think about food—visit a museum, attend a concert, go shopping, go fishing.

☐ Avoid looking at food-oriented magazines, and let the food pages of the newspaper go unread for a week or two.

☐ Plan a week's worth of very simple, easy-to-prepare meals, if you're the cook, so that you won't spend any more time than necessary in the kitchen. Or ask another family member to do the cooking for a few days.

☐ Go to bed early for several nights, and remind yourself that your growling stomach is your body's way of applauding your good work.

If it's to be, it's up to me!

Chapter 2
STARTING YOUR DIET

Beginning a New Lifestyle

Now you're underway — you'll be changing some of your eating habits and you'll be getting more exercise. Think about your new, healthy diet and the new sharpness of taste you'll acquire. As a starter, you might consider going on a crash diet for a week or two; the quick loss of several pounds might be a good morale booster. But remember that you're doing it only as a one-time thing.

Don't believe the myth that exercise increases your appetite; if you combine exercise with a good diet, it can increase your rate of weight loss by 10 percent over dieting alone. Start slowly and gradually work up to an exercise program you can stick with. As you increase physical activity, you'll not only burn calories; you'll feel livelier.

Making exercise part of your life

• **Think of exercise as spending calories.** Unlike cash, the more you spend, the richer you are!

• **Concentrate on small ways to increase your activity:** park your car at the far end of the lot; use stairs rather than elevators; get off the bus a block or two from your regular stop.

• **Regard housework and yard chores as calorie burners.** Work vigorously, using your upper arms and torso as well as your legs. Exaggerate your motions—reach higher, step longer, scrub harder, move faster. Do it all to peppy music.

• **Do your own fetching around the house** instead of asking someone else to do it.

• **Take the "pinch tests"** (see p. 23) to find where spot-reducing exercises are most needed.

• **Set a specific time for a brisk walk every day**—then TAKE it. Increase your pace and distance regularly. In bad weather, go to a shopping mall or museum to walk.

• **Take up aerobics** (vigorous exercise that improves the ability of the heart, lungs and muscles to use oxygen) and isometrics (exercise that increases muscle strength and tone by working muscles against each other or against a solid object).

• **Learn about yoga** (exercise stressing deep relaxation, proper breathing, slow-motion movements and sustained holds).

Making exercise fun

• **Buy** an attractive leotard or warm-up suit to make exercising seem more like fun than work.

• **Work on** your calisthenics while watching your favorite TV program or listening to the radio. Start by exercising during commercials and gradually work up to a full half-hour, but be careful not to get so engrossed in the program that you slack off.

• **Join** an exercise, dance or yoga class with a friend.

• **Dance** to some music around the house when you feel tired; this should pep you up.

• **Involve** your family in active games such as jumping rope, playing towel tug-o-war, running foot races, bicycling, running in place or swimming.

• **Laugh** heartily, at yourself if necessary. (**Calorie savings: 2.8 calories per minute.**)

Best exercise of all: push away from the table

Specific Tests for Spot Reducing

These tests are designed to indicate areas of obesity—spots where you have way too much flesh. Even those whose weights are ideal can fail some of these tests. They can help you by indicating the areas of your body you'll want to tackle most seriously in planning your exercise program.

The Pinch Tests: Pinch the back of your arm, between shoulder and elbow; your upper back, just below your shoulder blade; your midriff, halfway between your armpit and your waist; your abdomen, just below your navel; your hips, just below your waist; your thighs, about three inches below the spot where they join your torso. You fail if the fold of skin you pick up is more than an inch.

The Twist Test: Twist your nude body rapidly from side to side, before a full-length mirror. You fail if your superficial fat tissue does not move along with the underlying tissue.

The Belt Test: Measure your chest, at nipple level, and your waist, at navel level. You fail if your waist measure is larger than that of your chest.

The Magic 36 Test: Subtract your waist measurement from your height in inches. You fail if the number is less than 36.

Keeping up your energy

• **Exercise lightly** to counteract feelings of listlessness, fatigue and discouragement. Jog around the house, do some calisthenics or take a walk rather than a nap. These activities should increase your body's oxygen consumption.

• **Chart your energy highs and lows.** You can use this chart to help you plan your most active tasks for high-energy periods.

• **Consider taking multivitamins and a mineral supplement** to be sure that you're taking care of yourself. Women may need to eat foods that supply extra iron.

• **Keep oranges, apples, pears and other fruits on hand.** Their natural sugars are energy builders.

• **Drink vegetable juice** or unsweetened fruit juice after exercise. Don't head for high-calorie snacks!

• **Set aside a few minutes a day to totally relax.** You'll return to your tasks refreshed and in a positive frame of mind.

Expend ... so you don't expand

Kim Hunter

"My regimen relates to ME. I'll gradually put on weight if I consume more than twelve- or thirteen-hundred calories a day regularly. I simply keep that in mind and eat accordingly. Light breakfast (fruit, toast, coffee); light lunch (cottage cheese or yogurt); no between-meal snacks; and for dinner I'm able to eat most anything—even spaghetti—as long as I include a green salad and rarely indulge in desserts. A glass of wine and a bit of cheese at cocktail hour. And to keep fit, feel good, ACTIVITY—exercise and/or dance class."

Dr. Jean Mayer,

nutrition expert and author of *A Diet for Living*

"Your weight, like your bank balance, depends on how much you take out as well as how much you put in. It is far more difficult to lose weight if the only muscles you ever use are the chewing muscles. ... It is generally easier and far more healthful to lose weight by a combination of calorie reduction and exercise than by caloric cutting alone. *So don't forget to step up your activity.*"

Eight Sports: How Much They Help

Seven exercise experts were asked to rank eight popular forms of exercise on the basis of how much they help various aspects of physical fitness and general well-being. The experts were asked to score a given activity anything from zero votes (signifying no benefit) to three votes (signifying maximum benefit). A perfect score is 21, meaning that all seven experts awarded the activity three votes.

	RUN-NING	BICY-CLING	SWIM-MING	HAND-BALL/ SQUASH	TENNIS	WALK-ING	GOLF	BOWL-ING
Physical Fitness								
Cardio-respiratory endurance	21	19	21	19	16	13	8	5
Muscular endurance	20	18	20	18	16	14	8	5
Muscular strength	17	16	14	15	14	11	9	5
Flexibility	9	9	15	16	14	7	8	7
Balance	17	18	12	17	16	8	8	6
General Well-Being								
Weight control	21	20	15	19	16	13	6	5
Muscle definition	14	15	14	11	13	11	6	5
Digestion	13	12	13	13	12	11	7	7
Sleep	16	15	16	12	11	14	6	6
Total	**148**	**142**	**140**	**140**	**128**	**102**	**66**	**31**

James Fixx,

author of *The Complete Book of Running*

"If you run, you'll almost certainly lose weight, whether you change your eating habits or not. Because runners burn significantly more calories than nonrunners, women typically lose 10-12 pounds in the first year of running; men lose 20 or more."

Learning to Breathe Properly

Stand tall, shoulders back and stomach in, and inhale deeply. Hold your posture as you exhale slowly. You are increasing your body's use of oxygen and strengthening your muscle tissue. (This is also a good exercise to ease a hunger pang—remember it and practice it often.)

Madam Zitts
REDUCING
SALON
12 FLIGHTS UP
(355 STEPS)

GEO. CRENSHAW

"This is the reducing salon that's doing such wonders for me!"

Reprinted with permission of the Masters Agency.

It's Been Reported That . . .

. . . Rita Moreno always squats down or bends straight over from the waist to retrieve dropped articles; that George L. Blackburn, M.D. (scientific director for the Center for Nutritional Research in Boston) never takes an elevator for less than four floors; and that Henry A. Jordan, M.D. (co-author of *Eating Is Okay!*) has developed "inefficient office habits"—nothing is within easy reach, so he has to get up and walk around a lot.

One Exercise That's Bad for You

There's one exercise you should keep at a minimum—bending your elbow. Your elbow is one of the greatest little aids to weight gain ever devised. Flex it now and notice how beautifully it carries your hand to your mouth. Think how many times a day it bends, moving your full hand to your mouth and bringing it back empty. That wonderful, flexible bend in your arm is inextricably tied in with your eating habits, good and bad.

Calories Burned Per Hour by Different Forms of Activity

Standing still..100
Strolling..125
Driving a car..140
Taking a bath..140
Motorcycling...150
Doing light housework................................180
Making love..200
Bicycling (5½ miles per hour)........................210
Gardening..240
Golfing..250
Bowling..270
Scrubbing floors.....................................350
Playing tennis (doubles).............................350
Walking (3½ miles per hour)..........................350
Playing ping-pong....................................350
Chopping wood..400
Playing tennis (singles).............................450
Downhill skiing......................................450
Playing handball.....................................550
Doing vigorous calisthenics..........................550
Dancing (fast).......................................600
Bicycling (13 miles per hour)........................660
Swimming...750
Running (10 miles per hour)..........................900
Cross-country skiing................................1000

These estimates are gathered from several sources and are only approximate. You may burn up many more or many less calories per hour than those shown, depending upon how vigorously you perform the activity and upon your own size (the larger you are, the more calories you'll burn). Also note that the average person burns up to twice as many calories as normal for several hours FOLLOWING vigorous exercise.

It's Been Reported That ...

... Ed McMahon works out every day on a Dynavit machine; that Tony Curtis swims daily; and that Shirley MacLaine devotes two hours a day to yoga exercises and meditation.

Seconds count when you're dieting

Changing table habits

• **Before you eat, look over your plate of food** and try to add up the calories on it. This is your chance to remove some food (or at least to push it aside).

• **When you begin to eat, choose the food** (or foods) you like best first. Then you may be able to leave more of some other foods uneaten.

• **Take small bites,** savoring each one, and chew your food well (20 to 30 times per bite is not too much). Put down your fork or spoon after each bite and take a deep breath. Swallow one bite before you take another.

• **Set your timer for 20 minutes** and try to make your meal last that long. It takes that amount of time for your stomach to tell your brain that it's full.

• **Make eating more difficult and slower** by switching hands or by using chopsticks.

• **Or slow your eating** by using utensils for foods you normally eat by hand: use a knife and fork for your sandwich; cut your apple into small slices and eat it with a fork. You'll enjoy each bite, and you'll avoid gulping your food.

• **Use your napkin** frequently, and take sips of water or another beverage between bites.

• **NEVER have a second helping** of anything.

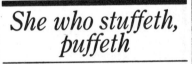

She who stuffeth, puffeth

Things to do instead of eating

• **Substitute other oral activities:** chew sugarless gum, an ice cube or a piece of thread *(really!)*; sing; play the harmonica (or try the noseflute—it covers both mouth and nose); call a friend on the phone and talk your hunger away; kiss someone; chew a toothpick; brush and floss your teeth.

• **Occupy yourself with a hobby or an indoor chore:** try sewing, cleaning a closet, working in the garden.

• **Get out of the house and away from the food:** take a walk; go to the library; ride a bike.

• **Make it impossible for yourself to eat:** try getting into water—a shower, a tub or a pool!

• **Look at yourself in a full-length mirror:** take this time to remind yourself that you want to stay in control.

Record keeping

1. Continue to keep written records of your eating patterns and habits, and make special notes of problem times, problem situations and worst temptations so you can avoid them. (See sections on taking a personal inventory, p. 6, and sample food intake record, p. 30.) Remember what leads to **D.I.E.T.: Did I Eat That?**

2. Weigh regularly (whether daily, semi-weekly or weekly) at the same time of day, and write down your weight. Keeping daily records works well for men because their weight tends to decrease consistently, while water retention causes women to have more frequent ups and downs. (Women may want to chart their menstrual cycles near weight records because of the water retention factor.) Note that some successful dieters urge weighing only once a month, to prevent discouragement. (If you do that, be careful not to weigh in and then feel free to splurge for a while before the next weighing.)

3. Keep track of your measurements to maintain high motivation; they may change more dramatically than your weight at certain points in your diet.

Know your weaknesses

4. Monitor your feelings about yourself, your new lifestyle, your habit changes and your gain or loss of motivation as you go along; record it all in writing to help yourself find out why you eat.

5. Note your weight losses as percentages of your goal. It's better to be even 25 percent successful than a total failure.

Face it: there are no valid excuses!

Dr. Barbara Edelstein,

author of *The Woman Doctor's Diet for Women*

". . . you have to learn again how to recognize when you are full. You knew it once, but you have forgotten it. Use volume in the stomach as an indicator. Start high; drink eight ounces of fluid, and think yourself full; then reduce it to seven ounces; then to six. Don't be afraid to drink with meals; that helps increase volume. Stop after a certain volume and tell yourself you are full. Repeat this to yourself enough times, and you will *be* full. The same holds for hunger. Re-learn what real hunger is. Learn it by the clock: 8 o'clock, breakfast; 12 to 1 o'clock, lunch; 6 to 7 o'clock, supper. Anything that you feel between those times is not HUNGER."

Sample Eating and Exercise Record

DATE: WEIGHT:
                               TOTAL CALORIES:
                               EXERCISE TIME:

Time	Food and Amount	Calories	With Whom, Where, Why, My Feelings	Exercise (Kind & Time)
6 a.m. - 11 a.m.				
11 a.m. - 4 p.m.				
4 p.m. - 9 p.m.				
9 p.m. - 6 a.m.				

Week in Review:
Average calories daily_____   ___ Achieved weight goal
Average exercise time_____   ___ Achieved exercise goal

Note: If you have only a few pounds to lose, you may decide not to spend the time necessary to keep detailed records. You may want to write down only the things you shouldn't have eaten, if bingeing or sneaking forbidden foods are problems for you. If you're not making your weight-loss goals, however, try keeping complete records for a time. It may be all you need to get going on the right track.

Reward and Punishment

The way you look and feel are the greatest rewards for following your new lifestyle. An improved figure, increased vitality, a better outlook on life—what more could anyone ask? When you've successfully reached one or two weight-loss goals, it may be time to treat yourself to at least one new garment to wear and enjoy. Consider a new tennis or jogging outfit, if you've taken up one of those sports as part of your exercise program.

But what if you're only human and have slacked off a bit? OK, so you're not perfect; don't give up! If you're angry enough with yourself to call some penalties, try to make the punishment fit the crime and do you some good.

THE BETTER HALF   By Barnes

"You should tell him there's a 'fat fairy' and if he loses 10 pounds he'll find a quarter under the scale."

"The Better Half" by Barnes; reprinted courtesy of The Register and Tribune Syndicate, Inc.

The best (non-food) rewards

• **Pay yourself** a certain amount of money for every pound you lose. When you've EARNED enough, spend the money on something special for yourself or for someone you love. Or make a donation to your favorite charity.

• **Gift-wrap something you really want,** and put it in the refrigerator as a reminder not to cheat. If you've reached a goal when planned, keep your present. If you haven't, give it away.

• **Put 50 cents in your EMP-TY cookie jar** each day that you stick to your diet. Do something nice for yourself or someone else with the money you've collected.

• **Buy yourself a pair of suspenders** (in a bright color if you feel daring). If you've lost a lot of weight, you can tighten the suspenders and your suits will still fit! If you gain some pounds back, you can loosen the suspenders and start all over again.

• **Be candid about asking your friends and family for praise**—it's one of the nicest rewards for any accomplishment. And don't forget to thank them for positive reinforcement.

Punishment to fit the crime

• **Write a check** to your LEAST favorite fundraising organization and give it to someone else to mail if you fail to take off the intended pounds. (And remember that you'll be on that organization's mailing list forever!) If you dislike this punishment, you can certainly give a check to your favorite charity.

• **Do an extra half-hour of calisthenics** the next day and every day after that for a week.

• **Eat a diet food** for breakfast the next day.

• **Do a chore you dislike,** with vigor.

• **Try on an article of clothing that's too small.** You'll be ready to diet again when you look at yourself in the mirror.

• **Stand naked before a full-length mirror** and tell yourself off. Then burn a few calories by having either a good laugh or a good cry.

• **Forgive yourself!** Forget your lapse and resolve to start over again.

The Worst Reward

Beware of the temptation to go out on an ice-cream or junk-food binge with your friends after a diet-group meeting, as a reward for attendance and good behavior. (Yes, we know it's done, but DON'T YOU DO IT!)

Chapter 3
SHOPPING AND COOKING

Grocery Shopping

It's been estimated that almost 47 percent of all food purchases are made on impulse and that a great deal of that impulse food consists of pastries, sweets and snacks. Think about one of your most recent grocery shopping trips. How much of what you bought had you planned to buy? And how many of those impulse pur- chases had little or no nutritional value? How many were fattening? In order to stop impulse buying, it's important to start planning ahead. You'll be able to shop less often; you'll save money; and you'll know exactly what you're going to have for every meal, with fewer tempting no-nos on hand.

Sample Daily Menu Planning Form

DAY	BREAKFAST	LUNCH	DINNER	SNACKS	TOTAL CAL.
Sun.					
Mon.					
Tues.					
Wed.					
Thurs.					
Fri.					
Sat.					

TOTAL DAILY CALORIES _____

AVERAGE DAILY CALORIES _____

Menu planning

• **Plan meals for a week ahead** so that you can do all your shopping at one time, avoiding quick trips during which you may pick up extras. This should help you to think about food less often.

• **Do your meal planning after you have eaten,** when you're not hungry.

• **Think of your planning as a challenging hobby** rather than a chore. Spend your time thinking up new ways to combine, prepare and serve healthful foods, instead of agonizing over "forbiddens."

• **Include the basic four food groups in daily menus** (see p. 36). If one takes care to watch calories and intake of fats, salt and sugar, these basic food groups provide a simple approach to nutrient adequacy.

• **Make good use of a diet cookbook** that contains tempting, calorie-counted menus and recipes, and watch for good ideas in newspapers and magazines.

• **Include well-balanced breakfasts** in your meal planning, if you're a breakfast eater (see p. 64), but cut down on your evening meals. You need plenty of energy to get through your day, but not much for sleeping.

• **Keep your menus simple and easy to prepare,** with add-ons for the non-dieters in the family.

• **Include leftovers in your plans** so they don't turn into "grazing" possibilities. You may want to save the leftovers in one container—and use them in a wonderful soup when enough has been collected.

• **Work in a few vegetarian meals,** even if you're a meat lover. You'll find them delicious and comparatively inexpensive, and they'll add fiber to your diet.

• **Build SMALL amounts of your cravings into your menus,** but only if they're not forbidden in the diet you select.

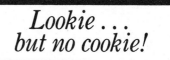

*Lookie . . .
but no cookie!*

Phyllis Diller

"It is very simple to stay thin. You just don't eat oil in any form, such as butter, etc. You eschew white flour and refined sugar. That leaves you fruit, vegetables, fish, fowl and a smidgeon of meat. You have to remember that some dairy products are fattening, like cheese and whole milk. These tips will keep you thin, but to feel good you must exercise; get sufficient sleep; drink no tea, coffee or coke; smoke no cigarettes; and cultivate the habit of happiness."

Suggested Daily Servings of the Basic Four*

FOOD TYPE	NUMBER OF SERVINGS	SUGGESTED SERVING SIZE
BEANS, GRAINS & NUTS	4	1 slice bread or 1 small roll; 1 cup unsweetened dry cereal; ½ cup cooked cereal; ½ cup cooked rice; 1 cup cooked legumes
FRUITS & VEGETABLES	4	½ cup juice; 1 cup berries; 1 medium fruit; ½ cup cooked vegetable; 1 cup raw leafy vegetable
MILK PRODUCTS	2 (3 to 4 for children)	1 cup skim milk; ¾ cup plain yogurt; ½ cup cottage cheese; 1 ounce hard cheese
POULTRY, FISH, EGG & MEAT PRODUCTS	2	Approximately 3 ounces, cooked

FATS: The better fats are mayonnaise, margarine and vegetable oils, except coconut and palm, but these can be overdone. Even the fat that occurs naturally in meat, dairy products and other foods adds calories to your diet.

SWEETS: Add sugar to your diet only when other requirements have been met, and then only in very small quantities. Sugar contains "empty calories," which fill you up but do you no good.

*A beautiful and informative full-color poster, "New American Eating Guide," describes the Basic Four and recommends foods in each category that may be eaten "anytime," "in moderation" and "now and then." It is available from C.S.P.I., 1755 S Street NW, Washington, DC 20009, for $2.50.

Stop that cheatin' eatin'!

Dr. Richard B. Stuart,

psychological director of Weight Watchers International, Inc. and author of *Act Thin, Stay Thin*

"In order to limit one source of 'hunger' during or between meals, make certain that you eat a variety of foods with different appearances, tastes and textures."

Calorie Comparison Tables

The following tables include calorie values of selected commonly used foods in the Basic Four, selected mainly to show caloric differences. Actual nutritional values vary; foods with comparable calorie counts contain different amounts of protein, fat, carbohydrate, sodium and other nutrients. You can use these tables to choose what to eat and what to avoid. Note that the left column in each section includes foods with lower calorie counts. Careful use of a good nutrition handbook, such as the USDA's *Nutritive Value of American Foods* (see below for more information), will help you plan meals with the most nutritional value and the fewest calories. If you are interested in following a strict calorie count, turn to one of the many available calorie guides; you'll find that their calorie counts are very similar.

Calorie counts for raw and cooked foods in these tables have been taken from (or in some cases based on) those given in *Nutritive Value of American Foods in Common Units,* by C.F. Adams (USDA Agricultural Research Service, Agriculture Handbook No. 456, November, 1975), unless otherwise indicated. The book may be ordered from the Superintendent of Documents, U.S. Printing Office, Washington, DC 20402, for $5.15.

An asterisk (*) after the name of any food indicates that the calorie count is taken from the *Calorie Guide to Brand Names and Basic Foods* by Barbara Kraus.

The following abbreviations have been used in tables.

> ## Dr. Jean Mayer,
> nutrition expert and author of *A Diet for Living*
> "Calories do count! Those three little words should be recited prayerfully morning, noon and night by everybody who seriously wants to reduce sensibly and successfully."

C	cup
T	tablespoon
t	teaspoon
presw	presweetened
unsw	unsweetened
sl	slice

Calorie Comparisons of Selected Beans, Grains and Nuts

BEANS AND PEAS
(1 C, cooked)

white, great northern.......189	kidney 218
lima 212	split peas.................230
	soybeans 234

DRY CEREALS (without milk)

wheat, puffed, unsw., 1 C......54	wheat, puffed, presw., 1 C....132
rice, puffed, unsw., 1 C.......60	rice, puffed, presw., 1 C......175
All Bran*, ⅓ C..............70	Bran Chex*, ⅔ C...........144
corn flakes, unsw., 1 C.......97	corn flakes, presw., 1 C......154
wheat germ, toasted**, 1 T....23	
**without sugar or salt	

COOKED CEREALS (without milk)

farina, ½ C.................51	
corn grits, ½ C..............62	
oatmeal, ½ C...............66	

SPAGHETTI, MACARONI
(1 C, cooked)

cooked tender, 1 C..........155	cooked firm (al dente), 1 C....192

RICE (1 C, cooked)

precooked instant (Minute)* ..180	white, long grain 223
	brown 232

BREADS, CRACKERS (white)

saltines, Nabisco*, Keebler*, 1..12	bakery, homemade, 1 oz. sl.....76
Wonder*, 1 oz. sl.............70	

BREADS, CRACKERS (DARK)

Rye Krisp*, 1 triple cracker....30	Roman Meal*, 1 oz. sl.........70
bakery, homemade, 1 oz. sl.....67	Wonder*, 1 oz. sl.............75

BREAKFAST BREADS

waffle, Aunt Jemima*, frozen...86	waffle, Downyflake*, frozen. . .130
	waffle, homemade.........140
	doughnut, cake type, 2 oz.....227

SNACKS

pretzel sticks, 10.............23	corn chips, Fritos*, 1 oz.......156
pretzels, regular, 5...........58	potato chips, Lays*, 1 oz......158

NUTS

peanuts, roasted, salted, 10....53	pecans, jumbo, shelled, 10.....96
almonds, roasted, salted, 10....86	walnuts, Eng., shelled, 10....130

PEANUT BUTTER

Peter Pan*, smooth, 1 T.......94	Ann Page*, 1 T............106
Skippy*, creamy, 1 T........101	

*Source: *Calorie Guide to Brand Names and Basic Foods* by Barbara Kraus.

Calorie Comparisons of Selected Poultry, Fish, Egg and Meat Products

CHICKEN

light (skinned, roasted, 3 ounces)...........................155
dark (skinned, roasted, 3 ounces)..........................157
half-breast (skinned, fried)................................160
drumstick (skinned, fried)..................................88

TURKEY (3-ounce serving)

light (roasted)...150
dark (roasted)...173

FISH (3-ounce serving)

flounder (baked)..71
scallops (steamed)..95
shrimp (canned)...99
tuna (chunk, canned in water)..............................110
tuna (chunk, canned in oil)................................160
cod (broiled)..145
salmon steak (fresh, broiled or baked).....................156
sardines (canned, drained).................................174
whitefish (baked)..183

EGGS (one large)

hard-cooked or poached......................................82
fried...99

BEEF (3-ounce serving)

chuck (lean, braised and drained, trimmed of fat)..........186
ground (lean, 10% fat, broiled)............................163
ground (regular, 21% fat, broiled).........................235
rump roast (75% lean, roasted).............................295
sirloin steak (66% lean, broiled)..........................329

PORK (approximately 3-ounce serving)

loin chop (lean, broiled)..................................339
ham (lean, light-cure, commercial, baked)..................246
loin roast (baked or roasted)..............................308
frankfurter (two, smoked, prepackaged).....................248

LAMB (approximately 3-ounce serving)

leg of lamb (trimmed, roasted).............................158
loin chop (trimmed, broiled)...............................342
rib chop (trimmed, broiled)................................362

VEAL (3-ounce serving)

round, with rump (trimmed, roasted)........................184
loin chop (roasted or broiled).............................199

LIVER (3-ounce serving)

beef (fried)...195
calf (fried)...222
chicken (fried)..150

Calorie Comparisons of Selected Fruits and Vegetables

FRESH FRUITS (raw)

grapes, 10 34	pineapple, diced, 1 C 81
grapefruit, ½ medium 40	apple, 1 medium 96
tangerine, 1 large 46	pear, Bartlett, 1 medium 100
apricots, 3 medium 55	banana, 1 medium 101
peach, 1 medium 58	avocado, 1 C, cubed 251
orange, 1 medium 71	
cantaloupe, ¼ medium 41	watermelon, sl. 10" x 1" 111
strawberries, 1 C 55	blueberries, 1 C 90
raspberries, red, 1 C 70	raspberries, black, 1 C 98

CANNED FRUITS (water pack)

CANNED FRUITS (syrup pack)

grapefruit, 1 C 73	
peaches, 1 C 76	peaches, 1 C 200
pears, 1 C 78	pears, 1 C 194
apricots, 1 C 93	apricots, 1 C 222
pineapple in juice, 1 C 128	pineapple, 1 C 168

CANNED FRUIT JUICES** (6-ounce serving)

grapefruit, unsw. 78	apricot nectar 107
grape juice 82	cranberry, sw. 124
orange, unsw. 92	prune juice 148
pineapple, unsw. 102	

**Frozen concentrated grape, orange and grapefruit juices vary in calorie count from canned by less than 5 calories per 6-ounce serving.

FRESH VEGETABLES** (boiled, steamed or baked)

zucchini, sl., 1 C 22	carrots, sl., 1 C 48
cauliflower, florets, 1 C 27	turnips, mashed, 1 C 53
cabbage, chopped, 1 C 29	brussels sprouts, whole, 1 C . . . 56
asparagus, cut, 1 C 29	beets, small, whole, 1 C 59
green beans, cut, 1 C 31	onions, 1 C 61
eggplant, diced, 1 C 38	tomatoes, 1 C 63
broccoli, cut, 1 C 40	corn, 1 5" ear 70
spinach, leaves, 1 C 41	acorn squash, ½ squash 86
	winter squash, mashed, 1 C . . . 129
	peas, 1 C 114

**In almost every case, calorie counts of raw vegetables and of canned and frozen vegetables vary from those of fresh cooked by not more than 10 calories.

POTATOES

boiled or baked, medium 90	french fries, 10 125
	au gratin, ½ C 145
	hash browns, ½ C 230

(continued)

RAW VEGETABLES
(often used in salads)

lettuce, chunks, 1 C.........10	mushrooms, whole, 1 C.......20
cucumber, sl., 1 C...........16	radishes, whole, 1 C.........20
green pepper, sl., 1 C........18	celery, diced, 1 C...........20
	onions, bulb &
	top chopped, 1 C...........36
	tomato, 1, 3″ diam...........40

CANNED VEGETABLE JUICES
(6-ounce serving)

vegetable juice..............31
tomato juice................35

Calorie Comparisons of Selected Milk Products

MILK AND CREAM

non-fat dry milk, inst.* (Alba, Carnation, Pet), 1 C..........80	
skim milk, buttermilk, 1 C.....88	
low-fat, 2% milk, 1 C.......145	whole milk, 1 C............159
half-and-half cream, 1 C.....324	heavy cream, 1 C...........838
evap. skim milk* (Carnation), 1 fluid oz.................24	evap. regular* (Carnation), 1 fluid oz.................42
	condensed milk* (Eagle), 1 T...60
yogurt, plain* (Dannon), 8-oz. container.............150	sour cream* (Axelrod), 8-oz. container.............432

BUTTER**

stick, 1 C................1625	whipped, 1 C.............1081
stick, 1 T................102	whipped, 1 T...............67

**Calorie counts for stick and whipped margarine are almost identical to those for butter.

COTTAGE CHEESE

dry curd, 1 C..............125	creamed, small curd, 1 C.....223
	creamed, large curd, 1 C.....239

OTHER NATURAL CHEESES
(1-ounce serving)

mozzarella* (Kraft)..........79	blue, Roquefort............104
Camembert 85	Swiss, brick, Edam..........105
Muenster* (Borden).........85	
Gouda* (Borden)...........86	cheddar 113
Limburger 98	

DESSERTS (1-cup serving)

frozen yogurt, plain* (Dannon) 180	frozen custard (soft-serve)....334
ice milk, 5.1% fat...........199	ice cream, 10% fat..........257
soft-serve ice milk..........266	ice cream, 16% fat..........329

*Source: *Calorie Guide to Brand Names and Basic Foods* by Barbara Kraus.

Preparing your shopping list

1. Attach a sheet of paper with a magnet or tape to your refrigerator door or bulletin board. Train family members to promptly write on it anything they have used up. Use that information when you make out your grocery list.

2. Make out your list according to the layout of your store. Then you'll go right to the items you need and avoid aisles that stock unnecessary foods.

3. Remember to check your recipes and menus so you'll purchase all the ingredients you'll need during the week.

4. Erase from your mind the thought of keeping snacks or treats on hand for drop-in guests—think more about socializing with them than feeding them.

5. Concentrate on staying in control. It's YOUR list; you're the one in charge of it!

When and how to shop

• **Shop at a time of day when your energy level is high** and you are NOT hungry.

• **Stick to your shopping list** unless you find a bargain on an item that's important to your diet.

• **Hire a sitter** or arrange a sitting swap with a neighbor instead of taking small children to the grocery store with you. You'll avoid the requests for treats and be able to concentrate on price comparisons and label information.

• **Take only enough money to buy the essentials** you need if you MUST run to the store between regular shopping trips.

• **Shop carefully on the edges of the store** where the produce and other foods that are good for you are usually stocked. The center aisles are apt to contain more prepared foods and more high-calorie treats. Remember that the grocery store's layout and display tactics place you in an "adversary position."

• **Ask a family member or friend to shop for you,** with a well-prepared list, if you have a very hard time resisting impulse buying.

• **Try to get someone else to put the groceries away** for you, or with you, if nibbling is often a problem.

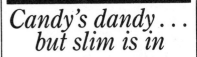

Candy's dandy . . . but slim is in

Shopping wisely

• **Locate a fresh produce stand or farmers' market** to buy fruits and vegetables in season. Products are fresher and prices are usually lower than in stores; and the shopping is more fun! Can or freeze what you can't use immediately.

• **Grow some of your own vegetables.** They'll taste much better than any you can buy.

• **Look for cheeses made from skim milk** to save calories; do your own slicing and grating to save money. Domestic cheeses are usually less expensive than imported ones.

• **Avoid convenience foods** and save both money and calories by cooking "from scratch." You might want to keep a few low-calorie frozen dinners on hand to use when time is really tight. Then you won't snack or grab the first high-calorie food in sight.

• **Learn to estimate the number of servings** in meats, poultry and fish visually, rather than by the pound. A lower per-pound price may mean you're paying for waste bone and fat. If you buy just what you need, you'll be able to avoid having leftovers.

• **Buy small-sized fruits and vegetables for snacks.** Larger pieces have more calories.

• **Buy whole-grain bread** instead of white. A piece of good whole-wheat bread can be almost a meal in itself (it takes longer to eat, longer to digest), while a piece of white bread can seem like nothing. Or try melba toast, which takes longer to chew, has fewer calories and is more satisfying than white bread.

• **Buy snacks in small, individual packages,** if you MUST buy them. Then you won't help yourself out of the big bag or box.

• **Leave junk food on the shelf** at your grocery store. You can't binge on food that you've left behind at the store!

A little of this and a little of that will make you big and fat

Reading labels

Do's

• Remember that contents are listed on labels according to the volume of each ingredient. If water is listed first, there's more of it than anything else in the product.

• Compare labels of dietetic foods with those of regular foods. If there is little difference in the amount of sugar, fat or salt content, you may as well select the lower-priced item.

• Look for "low calorie" or "reduced calories" on the label. The Food and Drug Administration has set standards for these items. "Low calorie" means that the product must contain no more than 40 calories per serving and no more than 0.4 calories per gram (an ounce is 28.5 grams). "Reduced calories" means that the product must be at least a third lower in calories than a similar item — and contain the same nutritional value.

• Make sure you know what you're buying in health-food stores. Some foods labeled "natural" contain more sugar, fat or salt than those not so labeled. (This can be true in your regular grocery store, too.)

• Look for foods marked "light" or "juice packed." They contain many less calories than those packed in syrup.

Don't's

• Don't be fooled by "no preservatives" tags. If a lot of sugar is present, no preservatives are needed.

• Never think that frozen yogurt has less calories than ice cream; it's actually just as rich! The difference is that frozen yogurt doesn't have as much saturated fat.

• Try not to forget to watch for the words "salt," "monosodium glutamate," "sodium phosphate," "sodium nitrite," "baking soda" and "baking powder." Be aware that each of them adds to the salt or sodium content, and thus water retention properties, of a product (see p. 51).

• Never buy a product without looking for the words "sugar," "dextrose," "glucose," "fructose," "corn syrup," "honey," "molasses," "turbinada" and "brown sugar." All are types of SUGAR, and even honey, highly recommended as a "natural" sugar, has a high glucose count.

Translating Labels: Sugar Content

Multiply the number of grams of sugar in a serving by four, since each gram supplies four calories. Now you have the number of sugar calories in a serving. Divide it by the number of calories per serving, multiply the result by 100—and you'll know the percentage of sugar in the product. For example, in one serving of a breakfast cereal:

12 grams of sugar per serving x 4 calories per gram = 48 sugar calories. 48 ÷120 calories per serving = .40; multiplied by 100 = 40 percent sugar in the cereal.

Translating Labels: Fat Content

Multiply the number of grams of fat in a serving by nine, since each gram supplies nine calories. Divide by the number of calories per serving, and multiply the result by 100 to get the percentage of fat. For example, in one serving of frozen, french-fried onions:

8 grams of fat per serving x 9 calories per gram = 72 fat calories. 72 ÷180 calories per serving = .40; multiplied by 100 = 40 percent fat in the french-fried onions.

For Better or For Worse   **by Lynn Johnston**

Cooking

Successful dieting no longer means denying yourself everything you like; it often translates as preparing foods differently. You can cut out many calories per day just by baking, broiling or poaching foods instead of frying them. More calories can be eliminated by using spices for flavoring rather than rich sauces or gravy and by substituting low-calorie dressings for the regular kind.

You'll soon find that you needn't serve the customary large portions of meat; you can prepare smaller amounts in tastier ways. Vegetables, salads, soups and fruits need not be looked upon as "fillers," but can be important and interesting parts of every meal. Fats, sugars and starches can be relegated to the bottom of the list in your daily intake without loss of flavor; all you'll lose is unnecessary calories.

Using recipes to best advantage

1. Compare low-calorie recipes with your regular ones to see how you can adapt the old favorites to your weight-loss program. (For example, remove half of the sugar that's called for in the old recipe.)

2. Read your recipes carefully to make sure you aren't adding unnecessary calories, and learn about substitutes for high-calorie ingredients. For example, think about using skim milk instead of whole milk **(calorie savings: 11 calories per cup),** yogurt instead of sour cream **(calorie savings: 282 calories per 8 ounces).** (See p. 38-41.)

3. Check your recipes to determine the number of servings they provide. It's better to prepare just enough for one complete meal than to have a little left over that may tempt you to nibble.

4. Follow your recipes exactly once you have adjusted them to the correct serving size, and DON'T taste as you cook. (You can eat a whole meal, right off the stove, before you ever serve it.)

Too many yummies lead to fat tummies

Low-calorie cooking

• **Thicken with cornstarch** instead of flour—it has about the same number of calories per tablespoon, but you need only half as much.

• **Puree vegetables** for a nutritious thickener.

• **Use eggplant or zucchini as a base for pizza** (no, you won't be able to pick it up to eat it!) or instead of lasagna noodles **(calorie savings: 170 calories per cup).**

• **Bake with rice crust** instead of pastry for quiches and one-crust meat and vegetable pies. Check in your low-calorie cookbooks for a recipe.

• **Sliver meat or poultry** and stir-fry with vegetables; a little goes a long way.

• **Extend ground beef** and cut down on calories by mixing 2 ounces of the meat with finely grated vegetables such as carrot, zucchini, potato and/or onion before shaping into patties or meat balls. Press the grated vegetables between paper towels to remove extra liquid, or squeeze by hand.

• **Add protein to vegetables** by adding flaked tuna to a mixture of cooked vegetables.

• **Substitute 2 egg whites for half the whole eggs** in omelets or scrambled eggs **(calorie savings: 42 calories per egg).**

• **Use bean sprouts or slivered vegetables with chow mein** instead of rice. And try spaghetti squash with spaghetti sauce instead of pasta.

• **Cook with wine** if you'd like to try a good meat tenderizer and marinade. The high-calorie alcohol burns off during the cooking process.

Low-calorie toast and sandwich spreads

• **Let toast cool before spreading** with soft butter or diet margarine. Cool toast absorbs less spread than hot.

• **Spread toast or bread with low-fat ingredients** such as cottage cheese or a combination of low-calorie mayonnaise and yogurt.

• **Use a tablespoon of jelly** instead of butter **(calorie savings: 53 calories per tablespoon).**

• **Chop or grind bits of meat** and mix with pickles, mustard and low-calorie mayonnaise or yogurt to make terrific open-face sandwiches.

Low-calorie salad dressings

• **Avoid calorie-laden dressings altogether** by using only lemon juice on salads.

• **Substitute tomato or vegetable juice** for high-calorie oil.

• **Add a tablespoon of mayonnaise to a cup of plain yogurt** for a dressing that will taste like mayonnaise but contain only about 16 calories per tablespoon.

• **Combine lemon juice and basil with yogurt to taste** for a dressing that's only about 10 calories per tablespoon.

• **Make a very low-calorie dressing for fruit salad** by adding a little orange juice, orange peel and honey to yogurt.

• **Add a dash of chili sauce** and some chopped green pepper, celery and pimento to a cup of low-calorie mayonnaise for a thousand-island dressing that contains only 40 calories per tablespoon.

• **Change your concept of oil and vinegar dressings:** using three parts oil to one part vinegar makes a vinaigrette dressing that has 91 calories per tablespoon, while using equal parts of oil and vinegar cuts the calories to about 61 per tablespoon **(calorie savings: 30 calories per tablespoon).**

Calorie Comparisons of Selected Dressings and Sauce Ingredients

	Calories per ½ C	per T		Calories per ½ C	per T
Salad oil	964	120			
Mayonnaise, regular	790	101	Diet mayonnaise	170	22
French dressing	513	66	Diet French dressing	125	15
Italian dressing	649	83	Diet Italian dressing	60	8
Tomato paste	108	13	Tomato juice	23	3
Tomato catsup	145	16	Lemon juice	31	4
Soy sauce	99	12	Cider vinegar	17	2

Little substitutions mean a lot

Low-calorie desserts and treats

• **Rinse canned fruits in cold water** to remove sugar-heavy syrup, if they're not "light" packed in juice. (These sugar-packed fruits are usually less expensive.) **Calorie savings: up to 60 calories per half-cup.**

• **Make your own fruit-flavored yogurt** by mixing 2 tablespoons of your favorite low-calorie jam with an eight-ounce container of plain yogurt. **Calorie savings: about 75 calories per serving.**

• **Serve yogurt or cottage cheese with fresh fruit** and a small amount of vanilla extract, or with your own homemade, low-sugar applesauce.

• **Poach canned fruits in their own juice or in wine,** and add a cinnamon stick or two for a spicy dessert.

• **Whip evaporated skim milk** to about the same consistency as whipped cream for a topping **(calorie savings: 646 calories per cup).**

• **Try frozen yogurt instead of ice cream,** and use unsweetened dry cereal as a topping instead of nuts or coconut.

• **Add a tiny bit of fat to cocoa** instead of using high-calorie chocolate.

• **Try reducing sugar** in your recipes by a third or more **(calorie savings: 90 calories per quarter-cup of sugar left out of recipe).**

While You're Preparing Food

• Put a bit of anything you MUST taste for seasoning on a plate, take it to the table and sit down to eat it.

• Have another person taste the food for seasoning.

• Ask someone to keep you company in the kitchen, both to help you with cooking chores and to keep your mind occupied so you won't nibble.

• Chew sugarless gum as you cook, instead of "tasting" your diet away. Or keep a drink of water, diet soda or tea beside you as you work.

In general, mankind, since the improvement of cookery, eats twice as much as nature requires.

—*Benjamin Franklin*

Cutting down on fat*

• **Cook soups and stews ahead;** then chill and remove hardened fat before reheating.

• **Use non-stick pans or vegetable spray** instead of oil or shortening to grease baking and frying pans.

• **Trim fat from all meats** and cut skin from chicken before cooking.

• **Saute foods in bouillon,** chicken stock or seasoned water instead of butter.

• **Brown meats under the broiler** rather than on the stove top in fat or oil.

• **Use butter salt or American cheese "salt"** instead of butter on corn-on-the-cob and popcorn.

• **Bake, broil or poach foods** you are accustomed to frying, such as fish or poultry. Poaching fish or chicken in fruit juice (especially apple juice) adds flavor without adding many calories.

• **Buy whipped margarine or butter** as a substitute for regular butter **(calorie savings: about 50 calories per tablespoon,** depending upon the brand).

• **Whip butter and corn oil, half and half,** to save on both fat and cholesterol.

• **Use natural butter-flavored granules** to flavor vegetables, without the calories.

• **Press cooked bacon firmly between two paper towels** to remove extra grease that clings to slices (if you MUST have bacon).

*Most of these suggestions for cutting down on fat will save you 100 to 125 calories per tablespoon.

Steve Allen

"If I want to take off several pounds quickly, I go on a mostly-fruit-juice diet for two or three days, although I will also eat a bit of tuna, some lettuce, some celery and such, so as not to get a too-empty feeling. For more casual dieting, I make low-calorie 'malts' in a blender, using a banana, an egg, honey, protein powder, ice cubes and a glass of water.

"A simple 'Chinese soup' is also helpful; my favorite recipe contains standard commercial chicken soup, water, celery and green onions, chopped up finely. I bring the soup to a boil and only then drop in the celery and onions, add a teaspoon of soy sauce and that's it. It's quite filling, especially with a little tuna and vegetable salad, but it's low in calories."

Cutting down on salt

• **Go easy on salt in the kitchen;** use only half the salt your recipe requires and add a little extra pepper or lemon pepper. Salt causes water retention and contributes to high blood pressure.

• **Always remember to taste** before you add salt to foods at the table.

• **Season fish and poultry** with a sprinkling of lemon or lime juice instead of salt.

• **Add vinegar,** a tablespoon at a time, to soups or stews to achieve a salty taste.

• **Use the freshest vegetables** you can find. You won't need salt to enhance their natural good taste.

• **Use foods with distinctive flavors,** such as mushrooms, onions or tomatoes to enhance soups, stews, meats, fish or poultry.

• **Use a marinade** of lemon juice, vinegar or wine with spices and a little oil to tenderize and add flavor to meat for an hour or so before cooking.

• **Use onion or garlic powder** rather than onion or garlic salt. The initial price may be a bit higher, but a little goes a long way—and you'll cut down on salt.

• **Try frozen vegetables** instead of canned ones. They usually contain less salt or sodium preservatives.

• **Combine meats with fruit** to avoid the need for salt. For example, try chicken with green grapes or peaches, ham with pineapple, veal or pork with apple.

Calorie-Saving Flavor Enhancers

Use fresh herbs and spices when possible; food tastes much better with fresh seasonings. You can grow many herbs yourself, even in small pots in the kitchen window. Store them all in tightly closed containers, away from heat, to preserve flavor and freshness.

With fish, chicken or meat: bay leaf, dry mustard, sage, marjoram, paprika, thyme, curry, garlic, rosemary, dill, oregano, chives, onion, green pepper, horseradish, lemon juice, nutmeg, basil, parsley, savory, pepper, lemon pepper, poultry seasoning.

With eggs: curry, dry mustard, onion, chives, parsley, dill, paprika, lemon pepper, tarragon, oregano, basil, marjoram.

With vegetables: lemon juice, parsley, dill, fennel, marjoram, thyme, basil, celery seed, bay leaf, pepper, lemon pepper, sage, savory, paprika, curry.

With fruits: cinnamon, cloves, nutmeg, ginger, coriander, allspice, lemon juice.

With soups or stews: marjoram, parsley, thyme, bay leaf, paprika, pepper, vinegar, allspice.

Making vegetables interesting

• **Steam** vegetables for better flavor, color and texture, as well as to preserve nutrients. Try steaming several together, starting with those that require the longest cooking. (Keep a bowl of these in the refrigerator for safe and tasty munchies.)

• **Season** vegetables with lemon juice or broth, herbs and spices instead of butter or cream sauce.

• **Marinate** raw or crisply cooked vegetables in vinaigrette dressing. Drain and add to salad greens—you won't need added dressing.

• **Vary** vegetable dishes by adding water chestnuts, mushrooms, chopped onion, green pepper or celery—all low-calorie enhancers.

• **Wrap** large, whole vegetables such as cauliflower, beets or cabbage in foil and bake with seasonings other than salt. Turnips, onions and carrots can be treated in the same way.

• **Heat** some vegetables in your microwave for a quick, nutritious snack. If you don't have a microwave oven, you might consider buying one as a reward for meeting your first weight goal.

• **Stuff** a baked potato with a main-dish meat or vegetable combination instead of covering it with butter or sour cream.

• **Mix** cooked vegetables with a little cooked pasta and grated cheese for meatless protein.

• **Bake or boil** potatoes instead of mashing them with butter and milk. Season them with dill, parsley, onion flakes or yogurt. Eat the skins, too, for added vitamins.

Dr. Barbara Edelstein,
author of *The Woman Doctor's Diet for Women*

"I prefer to keep a dieter's food simple.... If you are one of those women who love to experiment with new recipes (many of us do), then cook for other people, but get someone else in the family to act as the taster—and be aware that you're taking a risk."

Preventing obesity in family members

Do's

• Remember that weight problems can affect the whole family. If one parent is overweight, there is a 40 percent chance the children will be; if both parents have weight problems, the possibility for overweight offspring increases to 80 percent.

• Familiarize your family with low-calorie recipes and meals. Healthy food habits are good for everyone.

• Serve children small portions; they can have second helpings if they're still hungry.

Don't's

• Don't insist that everyone clean his or her plate.

• Never keep junk food in the house. Serve fresh or dried fruit, snack mixes, fruit juice frozen on a stick or popcorn as snacks, instead of sweets and salty treats.

• Try not to bribe or reward children with food. And never say, "You must be hungry," when the kids are grumpy.

• Avoid starting solid foods for a baby too soon. Check with your doctor; most now say that about six months of age is soon enough.

• Don't make meals the center of family social life—think instead of sports, games or just good conversation.

Chapter 4
STICKING TO YOUR DIET

Eating at Home

H ome . . . the danger spot . . . where food is always available, always easy to find; where you're probably accustomed to having a bite to eat whenever you want, in whatever spot you happen to be. Perhaps the most important successful dieting tip to teach yourself is to always eat in the same place (in the kitchen or dining room), sitting down. You'll want to keep all food out of all rooms except the kitchen or pantry. Some dieters try to eat alone until new habits become automatic, in order to avoid watching others eat large amounts.

Before you eat

• **Slow down your appetite** a little by drinking a glass of water or juice a half-hour before a meal or by eating a few crisp, raw vegetables.

• **Sip something warm**—a cup of meat or vegetable broth, a cup of tea or a drink of warm lemonade made by adding 2 tablespoons of lemon juice and a drop of artificial sweetener to a cup of hot water.

• **Distract your mind from food** by making each meal an "event," with a nicely set table, pretty linens, glasses and china. Plan to eat by candlelight sometimes.

• **Begin each meal by saying grace** or taking time for a moment of meditation to strengthen your will power.

• **Serve your plate in the kitchen or at the buffet;** don't tempt yourself to second helpings with bowls or platters of food on the table.

• **Use your food scale** and measuring cups and spoons to serve your meals, at least until you are expert at gauging portions. Cutting back an extra half-cup of the average dry cereal can mean **calorie savings of as much as 50 calories a day,** almost five pounds in a year!

• **Reverse the procedure** when you think you've mastered it—serve, then weigh and measure to test yourself.

• **Dish up a smaller plate** than you used to, but see that it is filled (it should hold at least three items) and looks appetizing. Fill in gaps with orange slices, vegetable garnishes, parsley or watercress.

The family dinner

Do's

• Keep the tone pleasant, making dinner a chance for the family to be together and enjoy one another's company as much as the food.

• Turn off the television set and put away the newspapers and other reading matter. You want to stop associating these activities with eating. Concentrate on the company and you'll probably eat less.

• Select topics of conversation carefully—don't make food and weight important subjects.

Don't's

• Don't allow the dinner table to become the arena for family conflicts.

• Try not to let children get the idea that the role of either parent is to eat a lot, or that eating a lot is equated with "growing up big and strong."

• Never let ANYONE act as the family "garbage can," finishing up the last little bits from others' plates.

• Don't force on children or adults the idea that they're insulting the cook if they don't eat everything in sight and ask for more.

At the end of your meal

• **Have a substitute for dessert** at the end of your main meal of the day: fresh fruit is fine, or you may choose just a cup of tea or black coffee. (Limit coffee drinking, though, or switch to decaffeinated coffee, if you notice symptoms such as fatigue, nervousness or headaches.)

• **Forget the "Clean Plate Club"** and the "Starving Anybodies." Always leave something on your plate, just to show yourself that you can.

• **Make up a special signal to indicate to yourself the end of a meal.** Put your napkin down, push your chair back and STOP eating.

• **Leave the table a little hungry,** congratulating yourself for your good sense and your strength.

• **Start burning calories by clearing the table** and cleaning up the kitchen immediately after dinner. There's an old saying that standing up for 20 minutes after a meal is good for digestion and keeps you from gaining weight, and that's just about long enough to do the dishes!

• **Try to get another family member to do the clean-up** if you can't resist nibbling on the leftovers.

Eating alone

• **Fix up your eating area** and make it attractive and inviting, so you won't be tempted to eat just anywhere. Don't just EAT—dine graciously.

• **Switch the order of your meals,** if it's convenient for you to eat dinner at noon and a light supper at night. If you work, eating the larger meal at noon, while socializing with others, may help you eat less.

• **Plan meals that need preparation time,** such as those that must be transferred from pan or container to plate or bowl and that require utensils to eat. You'll be less likely to gobble up your food.

• **Consider eating a quick salad** and then using your extra time to begin a project.

• **Never eat standing up** at the stove or refrigerator, making your meal seem like only a snack.

• **Put away reading materials** and other distractions. They make you forget what you're doing and eat more than you should.

He didn't make us to be garbage pails

• **Experiment with different kinds of music** as a background to your meal. You may find something that slows down your eating. And you may begin to associate a new kind of music with the new you—perhaps CLASSICAL means THIN!

• **Place a stand-up mirror on the table** and watch yourself eat. You may find that you're wolfing food instead of savoring it slowly.

• **Think of how important you are to yourself**—remember that you are dieting to please yourself.

• **Keep a list of projects** or neglected chores at your place to spur you on to activity after your meal. But don't go at them so hard that you feel as if you need another meal at 10 p.m.

What you eat in private shows in public

Dining Out at Restaurants

When you're eating out, plan your menu ahead of time if you know what the restaurant offers. Opt for a place that doesn't feature rich gourmet foods, an "all-you-can-eat" buffet or family-style service; look for one that has a good salad bar. If you choose a place that offers music, you may be able to dance off a few calories before you leave. Curb your appetite with an apple or a glass of milk before you go, especially if you'll be eating later than usual. You might even pack a "survival kit" with artificial sweetener and low-calorie dressing mix.

Ordering

• **Consider choosing a drink such as sparkling water** with a lemon twist or a diet soft drink, instead of a cocktail. You don't need the calories, and since liquor tends to deaden the inhibitions, you may eat more than you intended to.

• **Try to order first,** so you won't be influenced by the choices of others in the party. "Tune out" their orders and don't change or add to your own.

• **Select restaurant specialties.** Why waste precious calories on anything the chef doesn't do VERY WELL?

• **Order "a la carte,"** to get just the foods you want.

• **Try selecting two or even three low-calorie appetizers** instead of a full meal.

• **Think twice before ordering highly spiced foods**—they force you to drink too much, or to eat a sweet, in order to wash away the spicy taste.

• **Choose foods that require you to work** before you eat—unfilleted fish, crab legs, crayfish.

• **Order that one rich dessert** you're allowed for the month in the restaurant; there'll be no leftovers to tempt you.

• **Don't ask for a fork** in a place where chopsticks are appropriate—they keep you very busy and turn a little food into a big project.

• **Never order a combination dish** if you're not exactly sure what's in it. Ask about the preparation of anything you order, if you don't know.

Overeating is a social disease

"What are the temptations du jour?"

Getting the service you want

1. Be specific. Ask for exactly what you want, such as no bread or potatoes, a lemon wedge instead of salad dressing, a sauce or dressing on the side.

2. Tell the waiter or waitress, if you have trouble getting exactly what you want, that you NEED to have your meat broiled or that you have food allergies and may become very ill if exposed to certain foods. Restaurants never want customers to become ill.

3. Ask that the bread be removed from the table if no one else wants it (and it's a temptation to you).

4. Request that your waiter or waitress serve you a small portion (if your meal isn't served on your plate from the kitchen).

5. Ask that your plate be removed (of course you've left at least a little on it!) as soon as you are through eating.

Following your diet in a restaurant

• If you're served large portions, eat only half of everything.

• Separate the amount of food you're allowed to eat from a too-large serving, and make the rest inedible by covering it heavily with condiments.

• If you can't stand the idea of such waste, ask the waiter or waitress to immediately put the portion you won't eat into a bag to be taken home and enjoyed at another meal.

• Watch out for "food cues," and try not to be lured by them. Just as grocery stores stock candy near the checkout counter, restaurants often display desserts in prominent places. Ask your waiter or waitress to wheel the pastry tray away from your table.

I can eat or not eat: the choice is mine

Art Linkletter

"I try not to deprive myself of the 'goodies' I enjoy as a reward for watching my calories. So-o-o-o I order scrumptious desserts several times a week—and then eat only two or three good-sized bites. That's all I permit myself, but it's fun, like cheating a LITTLE."

Workday Lunches and Breaks

Studies have shown that two-thirds of Americans eat at least one meal out every day, and more often than not, that meal is lunch. Carrying your lunch to work or school is the obvious way to eat exactly what you want and need, but it's not always possible. There may be days when you forget to bring your lunch or haven't time to make it. And for many, there are times when the "business lunch" is mandatory.

Eating lunch out

• **Avoid restaurants that serve only "dinner" type meals,** unless you're going to eat heavily at noon and lightly at night. Look for a good salad bar.

• **Buy your favorite burger** or other fast-food specialty, but order it without the "special sauce" and eat only half the bun. Make your drink black coffee or a diet cola.

• **Take any food you buy on the street** to a place where you can sit down to eat it. Take the time to enjoy it.

• **Walk to a restaurant** some distance from your workplace instead of popping into the closest one.

• **Eat very lightly** if your lunch period is short and rushed, and plan for a nutritious snack later in the day.

Sandy Hill

"While I could never be happy with President Nixon's low-calorie lunch (cottage cheese with catsup?!), I find that tomato juice quenches both the thirst and the appetite. Whenever I get five to seven pounds over my ideal weight, I (try to) discipline myself to stick to tomato juice, water and cottage cheese."

It's Been Reported That . . .

. . . Angie Dickinson brushes her teeth often—and always after meals—to keep her mouth feeling fresh and clean. If you do it every time you eat, you tend not to nibble.

Calories in Selected Fast Foods

DAIRY QUEEN

Big Brazier Regular	457	Buster Bar	390
Big Brazier w/Cheese	553	DQ Choc. Dipped Cone, med.	300
Fish Sandwich	400	DQ Choc. Malt, med.	600
Super Brazier Dog	518	DQ Choc. Sundae, med.	300
Super Brazier Chili Dog	555	Hot Fudge Brownie Delight	570

Source: International Dairy Queen, Inc., Minneapolis, MN, 1978.

KENTUCKY FRIED CHICKEN

3-pc. dinner, Original Recipe. . 830   3-pc. dinner, Extra Crispy. . . . 950

(3-pc. dinner consists of 3 pieces chicken, mashed potatoes and gravy, cole slaw and roll.)

Source: Nutritional Content of Average Serving, Heublein Food Service and Franchising Group, June, 1976.

LONG JOHN SILVER'S

Breaded Clams, 5 oz.	465	Cole Slaw, 4 oz.	138
Fish w/Batter, 3 pc.	477	Fries, 3 oz.	275
Shrimp w/Batter, 6 pc.	269		

Source: Long John Silver's Seafood Shoppes, Jan. 8, 1978.

McDONALD'S

Egg McMuffin	352	French Fries	211
Scrambled Eggs	162	Quarter Pounder w/Cheese	518
Big Mac	541	Apple Pie	300
Cheeseburger	306	Chocolate Shake	364
Filet-O-Fish	402		

Source: "Nutritional analysis of food served at McDonald's restaurants," WARF Institute, Inc., Madison, WI, June, 1977.

PIZZA HUT

Thin 'N Crispy		Thick 'N Chewy	
Cheese	450	Cheese	560
Pepperoni	430	Pepperoni	560
Supreme	510	Supreme	640

(Based on serving size of three slices, one-half of a 10-inch pizza.)

Source: Research 900 and Pizza Hut, Inc., Wichita, KS.

TACO BELL

Bean Burrito	343	Taco	186
Beef Burrito	466	Tostada	179
Enchirito			
(a type of enchilada)	454		

Source: Menu Item Portions, July, 1976, Taco Bell Co., San Antonio, TX.

Brown-bagging it

• **Make carrying your lunch both fun and practical** by getting yourself a good-looking tote bag or attache-type carrier and a wide-mouth thermos for soups and salads.

• **Study magazines and newspapers** for low-calorie lunch menus and recipes and start a file for them.

• **Prepare and refrigerate your lunch the night before,** after dinner, when you're not hungry and have time to plan the menu carefully. If you're making sandwiches, put together a week's worth and freeze them to save time and sampling opportunities.

• **Take a physical fitness class** during the time you'd spend in a restaurant. Add to that a nutritious bag lunch.

• **Go for a run** or take a vigorous walk during part of your lunch break.

• **Take turns supplying lunch for two** with a dieting companion at work for fun, surprises and good, low-calorie lunches.

If you're not hungry, don't eat

Two Controversies

How Often Should You Eat?

How often a dieter should eat is one subject dieters don't agree on. Some say, "Don't ever skip a meal; digesting takes energy, and food spread out over three or more meals makes less fat than the same amount eaten in a big meal." Others say, "Never eat unless you're really hungry, mealtime or not." There are those who eat as often as they want to, but never to satiety, and those who insist upon exactly six small meals a day so they will always feel full. Take your choice ... or follow the rules of the diet you choose!

Should You Eat a Big Breakfast?

Another controversy concerns breakfast. Many dieters believe in breakfasting like kings, perhaps including all four food groups (see p. 36) in the meal, and eating lightly the rest of the day. At the other end of the scale are those who eat NO breakfast, saying that food eaten early in the day stimulates their appetites and makes them want to eat all day. Right down the middle go those who say, "Continue whatever breakfast habits you're comfortable with—your own body knows what's best for it."

*"My Lords and Ladies, until we get ourselves back in shape,
we feast on yogurt."*

Checklist for coffee breaks at work

☐ Remember that the only safe snack is a planned snack.

☐ Choose a desk as far as possible from the office snacking place, if you have a choice.

☐ Bring your own "legal" snack with you to work. Avoid eating a doughnut, a frosted roll or something equally fattening. A high-protein snack will help keep your energy up, but be sure to add the calories to your daily total.

☐ Remember that the "hunger" you feel at work may in reality be stress. Try an exercise break instead of a coffee break: walk briskly down a long hall or climb a flight or two of stairs.

☐ Take a moment to sit quietly and relax your jaw muscles. Anxiety makes the muscles around your mouth tighten and causes salivation, which makes you feel hungry. Let your mouth hang open for a moment to help relax it. (You may look funny, but at least you'll be THIN and funny!)

☐ Find a comfortable chair or couch, settle down, close your eyes and relax deeply.

☐ Use coffee break time for a personal activity, if you don't plan to eat—read, write a letter or make a list of things you want to do at home.

☐ Try not to carry change if you can't resist vending machines, or carry just enough to buy a piece of fruit.

☐ Never eat at your desk or other workplace.

Eating at Friends' Homes

Plan ahead! Find out what's being served, if the host or hostess is a good friend, or make an educated guess. Announce frankly to your host or hostess ahead of time that you're dieting, and ask for cooperation. If you know cocktails will be served before the meal, arrive late. Or simply save up by cutting some calories from your intake for two or three days —then "spend" them at the party. And don't forget to have a low-calorie appetite appeaser before you leave home.

Drinking and dieting don't mix

Holding your own

• **Pass up a cocktail** if you decide to sample the hors d'oeuvres, and vice versa. Give up both if you know the dessert has a "redeeming feature" and you've planned to eat it.

• **Don't sit on the sofa** in front of a food-laden coffee table, or anywhere else near food.

• **Bring your host or hostess a gift** of an appetizer or dessert you can eat.

• **Offer to help serve any part of the food,** so you can control your own portions.

• **Let your host or hostess know** if you won't be eating dessert, so it won't be dished up for you.

• **If you're served more than you asked for,** don't be afraid to leave food uneaten.

• **Look over the buffet** (if it's that kind of meal) and decide exactly what you'll eat. Serve your plate and move away from the table immediately.

• **Or stay away from the buffet table** and ask your spouse or a good friend to serve your plate with the best of the low-calorie foods.

• **Be sure to follow all the good table habits** you have so carefully established (see p. 28).

Dr. Joyce Brothers

"Use small plates. It fools you into thinking you have more food than you do."

If you're hosting the party

Do's

• Think of the dieters present and listen to their pleas for help, even if you're not dieting on this occasion.

• Provide non-alcoholic drinks for those who want them and at least some low-calorie hors d'oeuvres.

Ten Ways to Decline Offers of Food

1. Be "up front." Ask for cooperation in your diet.

2. Say, "No, thank you ..." Always start with NO and be explicit: "I don't care for more cake."

3. Produce a whole chorus of "No, thank yous" if necessary, until you're heard and believed.

4. Say, "It's wonderful, but I can't eat it now. May I take it home?" Or, "May I have the recipe?" Or, "You've filled me up. I love your coffee, though; may I have more?"

5. Say, "My doctor wants me to stay off that," or, "I'm having my cholesterol checked Monday."

6. Be eccentric. Say, "Today is the day I always fast."

7. Or, "I'm allergic to food. It makes me break out in fat."

8. Hold your hand over your plate.

9. And DON'T give in, once you've declined an offer, or you'll never be believed.

10. If all else fails, accept the kind offer—but ask for the food in a doggy bag.

Don't's

• Don't refill glasses or put second helpings on plates unless you're asked to.

• Try not to give the impression that you'll be hurt if anyone doesn't eat everything offered or served.

It's Been Reported That ...

... Arlene Dahl once said, "The feeling of hunger is indispensable to a successful diet."

Saying "no" is a learned ability

Staying on Your Diet While Traveling

Travel time may prove to be the very best time for you to start a diet or to stick to one, simply because so many things are different. Your routine is changed; you're in a new setting; you're surrounded by people you don't normally see. On the other hand, you may face greater temptations than those at home, and you'll have to be constantly on guard.

Plane travel

• **Don't travel first-class.** There are too many temptations, including better meals, better service and free drinks.

• **Order your food when you make your reservations** for a meal flight; a dietetic menu should be available.

• **Turn down snacks or meals** served at times you don't normally eat, or even at times you normally do. Airline meals are not noted for being really good, and many find they can pass them up.

• **Avoid alcoholic beverages.** They contain empty calories and they're big drinks—two ounces in a small glass. They may lower your inhibitions and encourage you to eat more than you should. Fruit juices are often available if you ask for them.

• **Push to the side of your meal tray** any bread, dessert or other foods you don't want to eat; cover them with the extra napkin the flight attendant will give you. Out of sight, out of mind!

• **Eat only on your own "normal" schedule** when you're changing time zones several times on a trip. You may have some meals at odd hours, but you won't be eating two or three dinners a day.

• **Do isometric exercises** on the plane, both to tighten your muscles and to keep your body from getting stiff and tired.

Work on temptations you can overcome!

Sticking to Your Diet

CATHY   by Cathy Guisewite

Auto travel

• **Carry "legal" low-calorie snacks with you,** especially if you are one whose juices start to flow as you back out of the driveway. Good choices are unbuttered popcorn, dry cereal, dried-fruit snack mixes, raw vegetables (in a plastic bag or in an ice-filled container) and grapes (which satisfy both hunger and thirst and aren't as sticky as oranges).

• **Play car games,** listen to the radio or sing songs to take your mind off tempting food.

• **Stop often at rest areas** and walk about, jump rope or play active games with the kids. You'll counteract the inactivity of sitting in the car and the change of pace will be good for everyone.

• **Read, knit or do crossword puzzles,** if you're the rider and such activities don't make you nauseated.

• **Have someone read to you,** if you're the driver. A good story can make you forget about eating.

• **Eat a large, late breakfast and a substantial early dinner** on long trips, skipping lunch. You don't need as much food as usual, and you'll probably save money, too.

• **Put off stopping for a meal** until you can find a place where you can get foods that are good for you. But don't drive until way after mealtime and allow yourself to get so hungry you'll overeat.

• **Pack a picnic lunch or supper** of foods that you can eat when and where you wish.

Special Tip for Bus Travelers

Be SURE to carry your own food. The regular stopping places rarely have fresh fruit or vegetables available, and there's almost never time to go elsewhere.

Vacationing

• **Try to avoid a guilt trip by being realistic**—plan only to maintain your weight (or even to gain just a few pounds) and resume your diet when the vacation's over.

• **Ask to see the next day's menu** if you are at an American plan resort or hotel or on shipboard, so you can lay your usual careful eating plans. Skip one meal, if lunch and dinner are both heavy meals, or ask for what you want.

• **Take advantage of your free time** by participating in any physical activities that are available.

• **Concentrate on the sociability,** entertainment and sightseeing possibilities of your vacation instead of on the food.

• **Don't stay at American plan hotels or resorts;** you want to plan your own meals and select your own foods.

• **Try not to linger for friendly chats** with others in the dining room when you're through eating—socialize somewhere else.

Business travel

• **Try your hotel room service** for some meals. You can order what you want, and the high food costs may influence you to order lightly.

• **Save up calories** and allow yourself a maintenance-type diet if a special banquet or party is planned.

• **Take diet foods with you** for snacks or to curb your appetite before a heavy meal is served.

• **Stay at hotels that offer exercise areas,** such as swimming pools, jogging tracks or tennis courts—or pick hotels near parks. Visitors' bureaus in some cities can offer help in selecting such hotels.

• **Stick to your exercise program** even though you're away from home; adapt it to hotel life and plan your time so you can go through it every day.

It's Been Reported That ...

... Carol Channing ALWAYS carries her own food with her, everywhere.

Chapter 5
TEMPTATION AND STRESS

Problem Times of the Day

Successful dieters are aware that HUNGER and APPETITE are not the same. Actual physical need is the basis of true hunger, which you should feel about six hours after an adequate meal, while appetite can be triggered by thought or sensation. But perhaps you really ARE hungry and do need food midway through the morning or afternoon or when you get home from work. Most diets can be adjusted to allow you to eat a little something then, and some are actually set up to include four, five or even six small meals a day. A fruit, a light protein snack or a small salad may make the difference between comfort and discomfort—and may keep you from overeating later. You can't eat at just any time, though, and there are a variety of ways to handle your cravings.

Between meals

• **Plan something to do** that is interesting and pleasurable, during any time of day that's regularly a problem for you—think of it as a "mini-break" and learn to look forward to it.

• **Do a few calisthenics or yoga postures,** go up and down stairs a few times or just stretch and bend; this should distract you and diminish your appetite.

• **Take five deep breaths**—and skip the food.

• **Do a small chore** when hunger strikes suddenly—tighten all the screws in the house, load the washer, sort the magazines, take out the garbage. You'll feel good about yourself for having accomplished something, and you won't have eaten.

• **Sip a drink of water slowly,** or use a straw. If chilled, fresh spring water is available to you at work, that's ideal. Otherwise, keep some water handy in a jug with a spigot for easy serving.

• **Lie down and relax** to find out if you're really hungry or just tense. If you're tense, try exercise.

David Brenner
"Never eat between meals and have meals only on Tuesday and Saturday nights. Avoid anyone wearing the color blue and never sit on a bus heading for Kutztown, Penn."

After work, before dinner

• **Enter the house by way of a door that doesn't take you through the kitchen,** if possible. Stay out of the kitchen altogether, if someone else is doing the cooking.

• **Do something, right away.** Open and read the mail, read the paper, change your clothes, take a quick shower or a short nap, take a brisk walk outside, talk over the day's events with your spouse or child.

• **Have at least part of the evening meal prepared ahead,** so you won't have to spend a great deal of time in the kitchen and be tempted to snack or throw together a quick, high-calorie meal.

• **Have something permissible available to eat.** When people are hungry, their cravings are usually for something soft rather than crunchy. Cold, cooked vegetables are "fool yourself" fillers; they seem like more than raw ones.

• **Have a warm, low-calorie drink** — a cup of tea or bouillon, perhaps — if coming in from the cold makes you feel hungry.

During the evening

• **Consider eating dinner late,** but only if it's a light meal.

• **Make the kitchen strictly out-of-bounds** after dinner.

• **Read a gripping suspense novel** that will make you forget everything else.

• **Be aware that some people's temperatures drop** in the late afternoon and early evening: their bodies cool, causing them to feel false hunger. If this happens to you, try a hot, low-calorie drink, or warm up by putting on an extra sweater or covering your legs with a blanket.

• **Don't allow yourself to eat in front of the television set** or in your cozy reading chair; stick to the rule that you eat only at your place at the table.

• **Go for an early evening walk** around the neighborhood.

• **If you must have a bedtime snack,** turn off the light and eat in the dark. Not seeing food seems to make it less tasty.

• **Take a long, soaking bath** to relax yourself and fill the time. Or get a family member to give you a relaxing massage.

• **Schedule evening activities** that will get you out of the house and away from the kitchen, such as meetings, bowling, tennis or cultural events.

• **Go to bed early** to shorten the evening.

At bedtime

• **Stave off middle-of-the-night hunger** by having a protein snack or a piece of fruit before going to bed.

• **If hunger pangs keep you awake,** lie quietly and relax your body, muscle by muscle. Think of the most pleasant thing you can.

• **Try listening to the radio** until you fall asleep.

• **Take ten deep breaths,** breathing as gently as you can. Then count backwards from 100 until you're asleep.

• **Read something** that will make you fall asleep.

• **Go back to bed immediately,** if you get up during the night. Lie quietly and wait for sleep to come back.

Make promises for just a day at a time. It's not too hard to avoid eating between meals "just for today."

Jayne Meadows Allen

"I often don't eat after 5 p.m. if I want to lose quickly. I go to a dance class, either ballet, jazz or tap, daily, and when possible, all three. The relaxation curbs my nervous appetite and helps me sleep well. Nerves make us eat too much."

Problem Situations

Many dieters try to structure their social lives around physical, cultural or entertaining activities instead of meals out or meals with company at home. They eat first, alone at home, and enjoy a tennis game, an ice-skating party, a concert or a play with friends, without the tempta-tions of food. It's called "eliminating temptation before it strikes!"

Holiday celebrations and parties involving food are parts of most of our lives, however, and a careful dieter can get through them without disaster with a little pre-planning and determination.

"They all ate at home!"

Reprinted with permission of Jerry Marcus and <u>*The Ladies' Home Journal.*</u>

Cocktail parties

• **Decide whether you will eat or drink**—don't do both. If you have a cocktail, avoid the hors d'oeuvres, and vice versa.

• **Provide your own non-alcoholic drink** inconspicuously, if your host or hostess has not been thoughtful enough to stock soft drinks for those "on the wagon." If a can of diet soda is too much to carry comfortably, consider a small can of vegetable juice.

• **Keep your hands occupied** so you can't eat. Hold something —a clutch bag, your hat, a pipe, your companion's hand—in one hand and your sensible, non-caloric drink in the other.

• **Don't eat as soon as you arrive:** look over the food to see what's best for you to eat. Delay ten minutes—then ten more.

• **Select a low-calorie item when you do eat,** or look for something you don't like much and won't eat a lot of.

• **Start a real conversation** about something you're interested in with someone you've just met—and talk; don't eat or drink.

• **Leave if temptations are too great.** Tell your host or hostess, "Sorry, but I have a dinner date."

"Instead Ofs" for Alcoholic or Soft Drinks

• Tomato juice with a lemon or lime twist, or with the seasonings you'd use in a Bloody Mary.

• Club soda or sparkling water with a lemon twist.

• Iced tea or coffee (black, of course). Or herbal tea, which has no caffeine (some authorities recommend caution in trying herbal tea—watch for allergic reactions).

• Canned beef bouillon over ice, or hot with a little lemon to spark up the flavor.

• Diet soda with diet tonic. Or diet tonic with lime or lemon.

• Fruit juice with diet tonic.

• Unsweetened fruit juice, about six ounces, with three ounces of ice water and a tablespoon of lemon juice.

• Powdered skim milk (about a quarter-cup) with eight ounces of diet soda. Using diet chocolate soda will satisfy both the desire for a cold drink and that for chocolate.

• WATER—best of all! (See sections on calorie counts for soft drinks, p. 79.)

If you do want to include alcoholic beverages in your diet, consider drinking wine with meals instead of cocktails before meals. The cocktail will lower your resistance so that you may forget your good resolutions about eating, and it may also increase your appetite.

Calories in Selected Soft Drinks (12-ounce servings)

Carbonated Waters
Sweetened (quinine sodas). 113
Unsweetened (club sodas). 0
Cola Drinks. 144
Cream Sodas. 160
Fruit Flavored Sodas. 171
Ginger Ale (pale dry or golden). 113
Root Beer. 152
Dietary Drinks (with artificial sweetener). 0

Calories in Selected Alcoholic Drinks

Beer (4.5% alcohol by volume), 12 oz. 151
Gin, Rum, Vodka, Whiskey, per ounce
80 proof. 65
86 proof. 70
90 proof. 74
94 proof. 77
100 proof. 83
Wines, 3½ oz. servings*
Dessert (18.8% alcohol by volume). 141
Table (12.2% alcohol by volume). .87

*Cut wine calories in half by mixing it in even parts with sparkling water.

Eight Reasons to Drink Water

1. It's basic to balanced nutrition (your body is 75 percent water).

2. It controls your body temperature through perspiration.

3. It minimizes dehydration from sweating and prevents overheating in hot weather.

4. It reduces stress on your circulatory system during sports activity.

5. It helps regulate your body temperature and controls fever when you're ill.

6. It's a lubricant preventing friction between the joints and muscles of your body.

7. It's filling, and it's cheap, if not free.*

8. AND IT'S SUGAR-FREE AND CALORIE-FREE!

*Treat yourself to bottled spring water and find out how fresh and delicious water can taste!

Holiday celebrations

• **Plan the holidays carefully;** structure the days so there won't be time to think about food. Include plenty of physical activity.

• **Concentrate on being thankful,** giving, sharing and decorating instead of on the traditional meals and treats. You can decorate the tree or set the table while others cook.

• **Hold down your expectations** of both yourself and others. You don't want your disappointment in anyone's failures to make you compensate by eating.

• **Try something active** that you've never done before on a holiday—take a one-day ski trip; go on a nature hike; organize a bike trip.

• **Consider taking your vacation at holiday time** to get away from all the pressures.

• **Serve a festive brunch with wholesome, low-calorie foods** instead of the traditional heavy dinner.

• **Consider having a "harvest dinner"** at Thanksgiving, emphasizing a vegetarian menu— a "new" tradition to start, since the holiday began with the harvest idea!

• **Rehearse your ability to say no** before joining a crowd when food will be served (see p. 68).

• **Eat a filling and low-calorie snack** before you go to a party, just as you do when it's not the holiday season.

• **Choose not to attend a big holiday dinner at all,** if you know you'll be unhappy. Your unhappiness may make you feel worse than the possibility of disappointing others by your absence.

• **Don't bake holiday gifts;** substitute other handmade items if you like to make your presents.

• **Try not to overindulge!** Consider taking a LITTLE vacation from your diet during the holidays, and simply try to maintain your weight.

After the Holidays

And if you get through the holidays without breaking down, think how much stronger your resolution will be. (If you can pass up Grandma's fruitcake, surely a supermarket doughnut won't be much of a threat!)

Problems of Stress and Tension

Stress and tension, both good and bad, are inevitable; everyone has emotional ups and downs. While you're under stress, it's important to realize that although you can't control all the events of your life, you CAN control the kind and amount of food you eat. Success-ful dieters realize that food often is used simply as a pacifier, representing security and comfort. They set up "plans of attack" for stressful situations, thinking, when they're not under stress, how they'll retain control when they are.

Coping with feelings of stress

• **Learn to say no.** Be sure you're not taking on more than you can handle; overweight people are often notorious over-achievers, trying to make up for what they consider their "flaws."

• **Check with your doctor** if feelings of stress and tension continue for a long time.

• **Talk out your troubles** with a friend, a therapist or the person you feel is causing them.

• **Avoid negative people.** There's nothing like a negative remark to destroy your positive attitude.

• **Slow down** a little. Relax in the warmth of a bath; the coolness of an icy shower; the escape of a nap; the peace of meditation.

• **Sit quietly** and think through the problem of the moment. Is it anger, frustration, depression? Once you're sure what it is, you can tackle it.

• **Be an actor.** Pretending to be happy and relaxed may make you feel that way. (But don't "cover up" all the time; it can lead to stress.)

• **Expect the best of yourself.** If you know you're going to have a stressful day, decide to at least follow a maintenance diet. If you slip even further than that, forgive yourself immediately and plan to do better tomorrow.

• **Try to see humor in your situation.** It might be funny to someone else right now, or even to you in the future.

• **Remember that you're in control.** It's not what happens to you that causes problems, but how you react to it.

Working off stress and tension

☐ Try to work off tension physically. Clench your fist; note the tension; relax completely and note the comfort you feel.

☐ Perform the same exercise with your forearms, thighs and the other large muscle groups in your body.

☐ Express your energy in something physical like running, chopping wood, pounding a pillow, scrubbing a floor or playing a hard game of racquetball with your toughest opponent.

☐ Use your time to do a favor for someone else. This may take your mind off your own problems.

☐ Take out anger by writing a letter to the person you are tense about.(But don't make a decision about mailing it until you've "slept on it.")

We "swallow" our anger

☐ Complain to someone in charge of whatever is bothering you. Try to solve the problem that causes the tension.

☐ Try to get away from it all by visiting a friend or going to a movie.

☐ Remember that people or events can't make you anxious or angry. You do that to yourself—so YOU can stop it.

Serenity Prayer

God, grant me the serenity
To accept the things I cannot
  change,
The courage to change the
  things I can,
And the wisdom to know the
  difference.

"I Should Weigh A Lot Less"

Actually, you "should" weigh exactly what you weigh right now, though you "wish" you weighed a lot less. Often we don't realize how the language we use and the attitudes the language expresses can create guilt and anger by carrying demands that can't be met. It's more realistic to say: "I wish I weighed a lot less, but I know that the reason I don't is because I eat more and exercise less than I need to." By removing the demanding "shoulds" that create guilt, frustration and anger, we can give ourselves a better shot at success.

Pre-menstrual cravings

- **Cut down on salt** during the pre-menstrual period to help avoid water retention, which is normal during those days.

- **Don't weigh yourself** during the week before your period will begin. The weight gain that is common then can be discouraging.

- **Save up calories** for a day or so, if you know you will be hungrier than usual, or borrow from the next day when you know your hunger will decrease.

- **Look for extra support** during the trying days. Understanding friends or family members can help you realize you don't have to eat more.

Hormone Shifts and Eating

Hormone shifts definitely affect eating behavior in women's pre-menstrual days. In one survey, 25 percent of the respondents declared that they ate more than usual those days. For most women, the cravings are for sweets. (For tips on handling cravings for sweets, see p. 88.)

If you quit smoking

Some people who quit smoking gain weight—about 10 pounds, on the average, in three months. Then they usually hit a plateau for about two months. Metabolism changes eventually cause weight loss to begin if the former smoker doesn't overeat. Taste and appetite will improve, however, so constant vigilance is necessary.

- Be sure to continue to eat non-fattening snacks.

- Take deep breaths when the urge to smoke or eat seems overpowering.

- Increase your exercise time by about 10 minutes a day to offset any weight gain that might be occurring.

- Try to decrease your food intake by 10 percent.

- Consider supplementing your diet with vitamin C, since smokers have lower levels of vitamin C than non-smokers. You may need more for a while.

- Chew sugarless gum, unless the chewing increases your feeling of hunger; remember that chewing does activate digestive juices.

Family pressures

• **Assume that people aren't aware they're hurting you.** If you find their comments and remarks cruel or offensive, speak up.

• **Have a private talk with your spouse** if he or she nags or taunts. Explain that you feel humiliated and ask for advice about successfully continuing your diet.

• **Remind non-dieting family members** that you can't do certain things with them because of your weight (if you're very heavy and really can't)—canoeing, biking, hiking, whatever the family enjoys as a group—but that you hope to be able to join them soon.

• **Invite them to join you in an exercise class** or a sport you enjoy and can participate in.

• **Ask them to remind you to drink more water,** especially if they say you're looking haggard. Water will help tone up your skin. (And let them know that your face will fill in a bit during the maintenance period.)

• **Realize that jealousy may be involved,** if the person criticizing you is also overweight, and suggest that he or she join you in dieting. But be careful to avoid an attitude of superiority!

• **And don't ever play the part of a martyr!**

Weight Loss and Your Family

While your spouse or the other members of your family truly want you to become the best person you can be, they may feel threatened by the possibility that you will be "different" when you're slim, energetic and in control of your life. Continue to ask for their help and cooperation and reward them generously with love, courtesy, small personal favors and often-expressed appreciation—anything that's NON-EDIBLE.

During and after illness

• **Ask** well-meaning friends who want to help with meals not to bring you noodle-laden casseroles, high-calorie desserts and sweet treats.

• **Appreciate** to the fullest a substantial weight loss if it's a side benefit to an illness. (A stomach virus is a sure-fire reducing method!) You may even be able to start a maintenance diet!

• **Don't try** to regain your strength through anything but nutritious foods; and don't test your ability to handle certain no-nos just to see if you're feeling well enough.

• **Remember** that food is not a tranquilizer or a pain-killer; it is NOT going to make you feel better, except as it works in your body to return you to health.

• **Keep** reading material or quiet, but engrossing, craft or art projects on hand during your recuperative period. You don't want food to be your solace and time-killer.

Use your recuperative period to improve your body, not to make it fatter

Changes in your routine

Some people are affected by changes in routine that are as small as the postponement of a meal. For others, weekends are a challenge. Vacations and trips are hard on many other people.

• Try to keep your hours of rising, eating and going to bed as similar as possible to those of your normal routine.

• Plan even more carefully than you do for your "normal" days.

Know when, where and what you'll eat for the whole day.

• Get out and try something active, both to burn energy and to keep yourself so busy you don't have time to think about food.

• Don't change the times of any snacks you may allow yourself.

If you work at night

• **Be prepared for a period of adjustment** to changes in meal hours or eating routines if you change shifts. You may feel unsettled (and hungry!) for a week or more.

• **Eat your regular three meals per day,** and eat only one of them at work if you eat two at home.

• **Change the order of your meals as you wish.** It may be more convenient for you to eat dinner with your family before you begin your shift, even though you have just gotten out of bed.

• **Don't urge family members to share your meals** if you can't eat with them at regular times. You may cause another person to have a weight problem.

• **Keep reminding yourself to enjoy the benefits of night work:** driving without rush-hour traffic, seeing the sunrise, having daytime freedom.

• **Try to find ways to improve your work** and expand upon your duties; even if your work is boring, you don't want to think of food.

• **Consider requesting a change of shift** or even a new job with daytime hours, if you just can't adjust to changed eating habits on the night shift.

Problem Foods and Drinks

Many successful dieters build their real cravings into their diets where they can. If a particular food is very important to them, they eat it, in moderation and by plan, instead of denying themselves and taking a chance on a binge later. Some prefer very small servings of a "real" food (rich ice cream), rather than a larger serving of a diet food (ice milk). Other successful dieters take a strict no-nonsense attitude toward eating. They say, "I'll do what I have to," and stick to their prescribed diets. Either way, it's important to deal with problem foods and drinks.

Forbidden foods

• **Contribute** to scout troops, hockey teams and school bands by giving them money as a donation, rather than in return for the candy or cookies they're selling. Remember to take an income-tax deduction!

• **Balance** your desire for a forbidden food against the "payment" you'll make in pounds on your body.

• **Visualize** the food itself; think of it in terms of so much fat and so many calories instead of in terms of taste and texture.

• **Insist** that sweets give you a headache or make you feel dizzy or disoriented. It may be true; refined sugar does cause negative reactions in some people—they build up an intolerance. (If you give up refined sugar altogether, it will probably take about three days to get it out of your system.)

• **Experiment** with "aversion therapy." Imagine the food spoiled and rotting or bug-infested. (This is not for the faint of heart!)

• **Think** of that forbidden food in terms of the distance you'd have to walk, run, bike or swim to work it off. If you do yield to temptation, then get to work!

> ## Charles Wetherall,
> author of *Quit* and *Diet*
> "I figure out in advance what's going to kill my diet (a party that's coming up or a business lunch) and make up a plan on how to handle it."

If you're going to compromise

Do's

• Plan carefully how the food will fit into your eating plan, if you're going to enjoy small, infrequent treats of something rich.

• Save up calories toward it for a day or two.

• Take just a teaspoon-sized taste of the food you desire so much, close your eyes and enjoy it to the fullest. Remind yourself that the rest of the food will taste just the same, so you don't need it.

Don't's

• Don't substitute something without nutritive value for something necessary for good nutrition—a piece of cake, for example, for a piece of fruit.

• Try not to buy the food until the day you plan to eat it. Stockpiling is OUT!

• Avoid eating until you've picked the time of day you'll eat the food. Then wait ten minutes—or thirty. If you still want it, eat it and don't feel guilty; you planned to do just that!

"Instead Ofs" for Sweets

1. Something vastly different in flavor, such as a dill pickle, sauerkraut, sweet-and-sour cabbage or stewed tomatoes.
2. An artichoke (the heart is said to have the sweetness of two teaspoons of sugar).
3. A piece of fruit or a glass of fruit juice. Pour unsweetened juice over the fruit and add a drop of Marsala wine for unusual taste.
4. Frozen seedless grapes.
5. A piece or two of dry, uncooked spaghetti (really!).
6. Coffee with a dash of cinnamon or tea with fresh mint.
7. Fresh fruit, whipped and chilled, with skim milk, for a "shake."

"Instead Of" Snacks, to Dip or Not

1. Thin slices of summer squash.
2. Cauliflower or broccoli florets.
3. Whole green beans, cooked one to two minutes in boiling water.
4. Sugar snap peas, whole or pods only.
5. Salad edibles, such as green pepper slices; carrot, cucumber or celery sticks; cherry tomatoes; mushrooms; radishes.

Good Dip for Vegetable Snacks

• Blend 2 t dijon mustard and 2 t lemon juice with cottage cheese; then add a little dill weed.

Chapter 6
PITFALLS ON THE WAY DOWN

Plateaus

Those first few pounds may have come off easily—but now you're stuck. Don't be discouraged; you've only struck a plateau, and several such pauses are normal during the course of a diet. The first pounds you shed were most likely water weight, but from here on, you're working on flab, which takes a little longer to dissipate. Remember that your body is adjusting to new fuels, just as your mind had to adjust to new attitudes toward food. Give it time!

When you can't seem to lose a pound

• **Keep a graph** of your weight loss so you can see the pattern in your plateaus as you progress through your diet. The line may sometimes level off, sometimes even rise.

• **Review your diet to be sure you're following it.** Remember that because you now weigh less than when you started dieting, your current intake may be a maintenance instead of a weight-loss diet. You may need to cut back even further.

• **Check your daily eating diary** for evidence of an extra portion or snack, an unnecessary dessert or drink.

• **Increase your activity** with longer or more frequent exercise periods.

• **Increase your water intake** by 15 to 20 percent for a few days to cause diuresis (increased excretion of urine) and possibly restart the reduction process.

• **Consider fasting** or going on a crash diet for just a few days to lose a few pounds.

• **Skip a meal and exercise strenuously** instead of eating. This "double-barrelled" action may result in the breakthrough you're looking for.

• **Stay away from the scale** and don't think about weight for a while. After two weeks or so, you may be pleasantly surprised.

• **Get out your tape measure** and use it. Your measurements may be changing, even though you're not losing weight.

• **Think of the important question:** not "How much did I lose?" but "How well did I cope?"

Finding support during a plateau period

• **Talk your problems over** with family members or a dieting friend and ask for some pats on the back for the success you've achieved. Don't complain, though, and don't become a "diet bore."

• **Attend some extra meetings of your diet group** and talk with the leader about your plateau.

• **Discuss your dieting problems with your doctor;** he or she may have some helpful suggestions for you.

• **Read about plateaus** in dieting books so you can better understand what's happening to your body.

• **Give yourself a lift** with a new haircut or a new hairdo. Since the first place weight loss is apparent is usually the face, you can probably expect a compliment or two.

• **Stand tall** and wear your new clothes proudly, so people will see the change in you. Their support may help you to continue.

• **Put on your old clothes, alone at home,** so you can feel how much thinner you really are.

Plateau Morale Builders

• Think of the pounds you've already lost in terms of something solid; lift something similar in weight—a five-pound pork roast, a ten-pound sack of potatoes, a twenty-pound turkey—and remind yourself you used to carry that much more weight around.

• Concentrate on the fact that you're not gaining, just resting on the way to your ideal weight.

• Keep in mind the fact that you have been successful. Think about how long it took you to gain your weight, and remember that the pounds that come off slowly are most likely to stay off.

• Envision yourself as a mountain climber, gradually pulling yourself upward and leaving pounds behind you as you move closer to your goal, the peak.

• Remind yourself how much you want to succeed. The harder you work now and the more patient you are, the less likely you'll be to let yourself go again.

Be kind to yourself

The Oh-So-Human Binge

Chances are, you're going to slip occasionally; most people do. If you do it only rarely, you won't cause yourself much harm; but if you find yourself "pigging out" very often, you will have wasted a lot of time and effort and not done your body any good, either. Pre-planning counts here—keep in mind how much easier it is to get fat than it is to get thin. If you haven't prevented the binge, you may be able to stop it mid-way. And if you go all the way with a binge, don't waste time wallowing in guilt; get busy and start making up for it.

Heading off a binge

• **Avoid overwhelming temptation.** A binge is usually triggered by one food; don't walk past it in the store and don't let it be in your house.

• **Think about WHERE you are hungry.** Is it in your stomach, or is it in your mouth or your eyes?

• **Find a friend** with whom you can talk yourself out of the desire to eat.

• **Force yourself to wait a bit before you give in.** Set a timer for five or ten minutes, and remember that the difference between winners and losers in dieting is that the losers give in.

• **Stretch your imagination** to avoid temptation. Picture the salted nuts as little globs of hard fat, the chocolate sauce as greasy gravy over your ice cream. (See p. 87 for more tips.) Or see that piece of cake, pie or candy glued to your thigh . . . your hip . . . your arm . . . your chin.

• **Distract yourself;** change your surroundings and your activity. (See p. 28.) A change of pace may let your craving subside and put you back on track.

• **Yell "STOP"** when you head for the source of food. Scold yourself as if you were a naughty child.

• **Take a few minutes to dream** about how you will look when you reach your goal weight.

*He who indulges,
bulges*

Controlling a binge

• **Make yourself sit down at the table** with your binge food, and eat it on the least attractive plate you have, with plastic utensils. Serve yourself generously so you won't take a little now, go back for more in a moment . . . and then even a little more.

• **Try eating just a tiny bit of** a binge food and see if you can savor it enough to stop there.

• **Substitute a crunchy pickle** or raw vegetable for the fattening, "soft and sweet" food you crave. Or stave off hunger with a can of vegetables. A 14½-ounce can of asparagus has only 74 calories; a piece of Danish pastry contains 274 calories. **(Calorie savings: 200 calories per serving.)**

• **Force yourself to put your fork down** and walk out of the room. A binge is controllable—when you stop, it's over.

• **Maintain at least some discipline,** if you're eating your real binge food, by not eating the WHOLE bagful or boxful. Or count the number of chips or cookies you eat. Leaving even just a little will make bouncing back the next day easier.

Making up for a binge

• **Plan your next few meals immediately.** Try to estimate the number of calories you've eaten and decide how you can cut down to make up for them.

• **Establish a specific "post-binge day" diet** and exercise program to make up for the extra calories you've eaten and to discourage future binges. (If you hate sit-ups, start off your post-binge day with ten or twenty; if you aren't too keen on All Bran or Puffed Wheat, schedule one of them for post-binge day breakfast.)

• **Work off more of the calories** with specific kinds of exercise. (See p. 25.)

• **Learn what you can from your slip.** Check your eating diary to find what causes a binge for you, and plan to do what you can to avoid it another time.

• **Forgive yourself!** It's water over the dam.

Cheaters never lose (and losers hardly ever cheat!)

Dr. Joyce A. Bockar,

author of *The Last Best Diet Book*

"If you plan to cheat, if you plan a binge, then the guilt is removed. You can enjoy the binge, and you will be more likely to be able to go back on the diet refreshed and ready for another three weeks of dieting. This concept is called binge-and-starve, and I use it for dieting and maintenance. You shouldn't use it until you have enough dieting behind you to make you confident that you can lose some weight, that you can diet. For most of us, this point is reached after a loss of ten pounds or so. This means that once you lose ten pounds, and at every ten-pound interval, it is perfectly acceptable to go off your diet for one or two days and go right back on it the third."

Backsliding

When you've almost achieved your goal, it's easy to slip right back into the bad old ways and, before you know it, back into the fat old days. However, if you keep track of the way your clothes fit and check the scale regularly, this needn't happen.

If your belt seems a little tight or the scale creeps up a pound or two, take time to examine what's going on in your life. Are you in a stressful situation that you're handling with food instead of calm reason? Do you think you are too busy to get the exercise you should? Or are you just getting smug and lazy and slipping back into bad habits? Be honest with yourself; determine what's really happening. Then decide what you're going to do about it.

"Yo-yo syndrome: the rhythm method of girth control."
— *Dr. Jean Mayer*
(obesity and nutrition specialist)

Paraphrase

The Lord is my Shepherd; I shall not want.
He maketh me to lie down and do push ups.
He giveth me Hollywood bread.
He restoreth my waistline.
He leadeth me past the refrigerator for my own sake.
He maketh me partake of green beans instead of potatoes.
He leadeth me past the pizzeria.
Yea, though I walk through the bakery,
I shall not falter, for Thou art with me.
Thy Tab and Thy Fresca they comfort me.
Thou preparest a diet for me in the presence of mine enemies.
Thou anointest my lettuce with lo-cal oil.
My cup will not overflow.
Surely, Rye-Krisp and D-Zerta shall follow me
All the days of my life.
And I shall live with the pangs of hunger forever.

— Source Unknown

When you catch yourself backsliding

• **Concentrate** not on what's WRONG with you and how you blew it, but on what's RIGHT with you. You've done a lot of good, hard work, and you can do it again.

• **Admit** that it's easier to take care of five pounds now than it will be to take care of thirty pounds in a few months. Remind yourself that a month's weight loss can be gained back over a weekend.

• **Locate** a dressing room with fluorescent lights and a three-way mirror and take a good, long look at yourself from every angle. You'll know what you have to do.

• **Examine** and, if necessary, adjust your diet and your exercise plan.

• **Quit** slacking off—take control of your life again!

• **Try** (again!) to remember to center family and social activities around sports, cultural events or anything other than eating.

Dr. Frank Field,

author of *Take It Off with Frank*

"If you find that you've cheated in spite of your excellent intentions, don't give up. I'm the first to admit that I indulged myself while dieting —not once but three or four times. Even so, I managed to return to the diet and made it work. The trick is to return immediately to your diet regimen—and to forgive yourself, *completely,* for that one mistake. Consider it as an exceptional event, and it's more likely to become one."

"I Can't Resist (Temptation Food)"

If you're not eating (your temptation food) right now, didn't eat it for breakfast, and don't plan to drop what you're doing to eat it in 10 minutes, you CAN resist it . . . just not all the time! It's important to remember that these negative words and thoughts can upset you and reduce your chances of dieting successfully. They can also provide a convenient excuse for a binge. Avoid putting yourself down and you'll be better able to deal with your greatest temptations.

You don't have to satisfy the hunger!

Chapter 7

MAINTAINING YOUR IDEAL WEIGHT

The New You

Lucky you—now you're down there. You have the satisfaction of knowing you've reached your goal; you look better, feel better and know you've probably increased your chances for long-term good health. You'll need to accept responsibility for continued effort; and remember you most likely have ahead of you a lifetime of continuous attention to your eating habits.

So You're Not a Perfect "10"

Your new weight may not have turned you into a perfect movie-star "10," but if you've firmed up as you've slimmed down, you can be satisfied with yourself. You'll never again have to think of yourself as "fat," "gross" or "chunky."

Staying on track

• **Weigh yourself** daily or weekly, as you prefer, but do watch your weight carefully. It's for maintenance that you might want to have a really accurate scale; a pound or two can be significant now.

• **Adjust your maintenance diet** if your weight "yo-yos" up and down or if you go over your ideal weight by more than a few pounds. Limit some foods if you must—starches, for example.

• **Go back to your reducing diet**, if necessary, and start over by adding foods back to it one at a time. Wait between additions to be sure a new one doesn't cause you to gain weight again.

• **Go back to your record keeping** if you begin to gain. Many successful dieters keep records for a week of every month, just to check on themselves.

• **Continue to plan carefully** for parties, holidays and vacations. Estimate a reasonable weight gain, if it seems that you won't hold your own on a particular occasion, but go back to your diet and stay on it until you reach your ideal weight again.

• **Check your table habits** occasionally (see p. 28) to be sure you're still following them.

• **Concentrate on having fun** in areas that don't involve food; spend your money to do something other than EAT.

Maintenance plans that have worked for some

• **Consider alternating diet days with normal eating days,** if you want to splurge a bit.

• **Fast for a day occasionally,** but be sure to plan day-before and day-after meals carefully, including plenty of fruits and vegetables.

• **Try a liquid diet** one day a week.

Maintenance: Daily Calorie Requirements

Plan your maintenance diet as carefully as you planned your reducing diet. To know the number of calories you should eat, multiply your ideal weight by:
• 12, if you're sedentary.
• 15, if you're moderately active.
• 18, if you're very active.

It's Been Reported That . . .

. . . Eddie Rabbitt maintains his 6-foot, 3-inch, 195-pound frame by jogging and jumping rope when he's on the road.

Maintenance Don't's

• **Don't** take your thinness for granted; believe what you see in the mirror, on the tape measure and on the scale, and appreciate it.

• **Don't** be complacent and let yourself get careless about your eating habits.

• **Don't** lie about your eating habits or your weight to your friends, your doctor, your diet-group leader—or yourself.

• **Don't** let yourself become bored with your maintenance diet. Keep collecting low-calorie menus and recipes, and spice things up a bit if you begin to be tired of your meals.

• **Don't** keep your old, large-sized clothes "just in case." You're committing yourself to failure if you do.

• **Don't** ever accept the following roles or titles again: "the world's greatest cook," "Big Mama" or "Big Daddy."

• **Don't** let your fantasies of a new, thin life overcome your sense of reality. You can't expect instant love, social success and career advancement because of weight loss alone—you have to earn them. You have proven to yourself, though, that you can succeed at what you attempt, so try anything you want to!

Living "thin," when you've lost a lot

• **Notice your physical movements.** Don't waddle, roll and pitch like a fat person—walk erectly, with an even stride. Watch your sitting and standing postures, too; your knees probably don't have to be as far apart as you used to place them.

• **Beware of old "fat" habits.** Don't automatically turn sideways to get through a narrow space or into a small chair.

• **Make "thin" responses to everyday situations.**

There IS room for you on the elevator or the sofa, and you CAN do physical things you used to not be able to do.

• **Remember the wounding remarks and taunts** people used to make about your size or weight. Rejoice in the fact that they can't do that anymore; you've changed.

• **Try to keep a positive attitude.** Don't let yourself feel what Judith Thurman expressed in a *MS* magazine article: "I'm never too thin to feel fat."

Living "thin," when you've lost a few pounds

• **Spend more money than you normally would for a new outfit.** Enjoy it in your new slimness; know your new size and tell it to sales clerks with pride.

• **Keep noticing how your size has changed.** You can zip pants without holding your breath and button shirts or blouses without stretching the material.

• **Be proud of your new figure.** Go back to that dressing room with the fluorescent lights and the three-sided mirror—and LOOK—and GLOAT!

• **Insist that you should never think of yourself as overweight.** You've reached your goal, you're thin and you'll stay that way.

It's Been Reported That . . .

. . . Larry (formerly "Fats") Goldberg, a pizza manufacturer who lost well over a hundred pounds, maintains his weight by eating whatever he likes on two days a week and rigidly dieting on the other five.

Rewards and uplifts

• **Pay attention to the small, ordinary, good things in life** other than food—the creature comfort of a hot shower, the beauty of good weather, the satisfaction in the completion of a task, the thrill of a compliment.

• **Continue to reward yourself in small ways** for all the things you accomplish—but NEVER with food.

• **Keep your spirits up** by occasionally giving yourself a "day at a spa" at home, including complete loving care of your body and rest and relaxation.

Love yourself

Remember When You Were Just a Few Pounds Overweight, and . . .

—you sucked in your stomach whenever you saw anyone looking at you?

—you glanced with envy at every slim person you saw?

—you didn't really believe people who said, "You look great today"?

—you were ashamed to tell anyone what size clothes you wore?

—you had to worry about what to wear every day, because some of your clothes made you look terrible and others just didn't fit anymore?

My loss is my gain

Or Remember When You Were Way Overweight, and . . .

—you used to check the weight capacity of an elevator before getting on?

—you avoided going to some stores because you couldn't get down the aisles without turning sideways?

—you avoided certain theaters because the seats were so narrow you had to sit sideways?

—you always tried to use a restroom stall designed for the handicapped, because they're so much more roomy?

—you tried to avoid airplane, train or bus restrooms altogether?

—you looked over all the chairs in a room to find one that you could fit into and that you were sure you wouldn't break? And hoped against hope that you'd be able to get a roomy loveseat or couch all to yourself?

Handling the Old Temptations

It's important to be aware that your "sensitivity" to food may always be with you. There are very few dieters who adjust totally to new eating habits during the time they're on reducing diets and, after reaching ideal weight, maintain it almost without effort. (They're probably the ones who had the least to lose!) Many others do well most of the time, but must identify certain foods or situations which are liable to cause problems. Other dieters have problems to battle every day and must constantly review and be aware of the habits and attitudes they worked so hard to maintain during their dieting days. You know which type of person you are—take appropriate action!

Reminders

1. Have lots of pictures of the new you taken by friends and family members. Keep them around where you can enjoy looking at them often.

2. Keep another picture handy as a reminder—one of you at your worst.

3. Change the cartoons and diet stickers on your refrigerator often, so that you don't forget to look at them and remember that you're not going to backslide.

4. Get out any of the literature you found helpful while you were dieting and re-read it before the holidays or whenever you expect to encounter temptation.

5. Continue to gather new dieting material. You'll still appreciate a new dieting tip, even though you don't need it as much as you once did.

6. If you're tempted to backslide, imagine yourself as a person you admire tremendously (perhaps the one you held up to yourself as a model during your diet). He or she would NEVER cheat on a maintenance diet, and you know it!

A Warning

Responses to foods change with time. A food that presented no problems last year or last month may be a real danger tomorrow!

Hunger pangs checklist

☐ Ask yourself (when you're tempted to overeat), "Do I really want this, or would I rather be thin?"

☐ Think of your hunger as drawing on stored food—something GOOD.

☐ Think of food not as FORBIDDEN, but as something you can decide about.

☐ Consider food as fuel (as in eating to live) rather than as a source of pleasure (as in living to eat).

☐ Don't ever carry food with you in the car, in your purse or in your briefcase. And don't stockpile snacks anywhere.

☐ Avoid eating cues in conversation. Don't "butter up" people, put "all your eggs in one basket" or describe a task as "easy as pie."

☐ Don't torture yourself by watching Julia Child or other famous chefs on television. Also avoid reruns of *Animal House* (food fights!), *Who's Killing the Great Chefs of Europe* (dessert scene, especially!) and old Mary Tyler Moore shows in which Betty White performed her home economist's part so well.

☐ Try not to eat even the "free" foods of your former diet at odd times of day to hold off hunger. Just don't eat at all, unless it's time to. You've changed your habits, remember?

☐ Continue to eat slowly (as you have been doing since you started this diet) and remind yourself about the many positive changes you've already made.

☐ Continue to think about cutting the amount you eat, rather than the kinds of foods. Eat with your family and enjoy the foods they do, but eat less than they do.

Returning to your diet group

• **Try to stay involved in some way** with your diet group, even after you no longer need the support. A paid position or volunteer work with the organization will keep you in touch and make it easier to return as an active member, if you ever wish to.

• **Keep in touch with friends you made in the group;** see them as often as you can and talk about dieting and maintenance with them.

• **Don't be embarrassed to return to your diet group** if you begin to gain weight again. Be happy that the group is there for you. Go back and make new resolutions to lose and KEEP the pounds off.

The People in Your Life

Your relationships with friends and family members have probably been undergoing subtle changes all through your diet. You've no doubt already redefined LOVE, realizing that whatever else it consists of, it has nothing at all to do with FOOD. If you haven't, now's the time to do it.

It's time, too, to come to terms with all your old defenses and to quit using them. The excuses you used to make to get out of doing things you didn't want to do, going places you didn't want to go and seeing people you didn't want to see just won't hold up any more. You look fine now and your energy level is high, because your weight is right and you're in good health. People expect more of a "normal" person than they used to expect of you, and you'll have to deal with that fact.

"Friends" who don't help

• **Don't look to your over-weight friends** to help you maintain your ideal weight. They may be jealous of you; they may try to tempt you to backslide. The chances that they'll offer congratulations and support are nil.

• **Make a list** of those who caution you about being "too thin" and who try to feed you back into fatness. Be on guard when you're with them.

• **See as little as possible** of those whom you feel will really cause you problems. Your own good health and well-being are most important.

• **Remember that you can't blame your friends** for your own actions. Whatever others are doing to you, for you or about you, they're NOT going to eat for you—you do that for yourself.

• **Smile and bite your tongue** when a friend says, "I wish I could lose weight and keep it off as easily as you do." Nobody who hasn't gone through it all will ever really understand.

"No one can make you feel inferior without your consent."
—*Eleanor Roosevelt*

New relationships with others

• **Train yourself to say NO,** simply and firmly, when it's appropriate. You don't have to do anything you don't want to, and you don't have to make excuses.

• **Learn to accept compliments** with a simple "Thank you." But realize that compliments about your weight loss will stop; people will get used to the slim you and forget that you ever deserved praise for sticking to a diet. And new friends will never know you were overweight.

• **Take off the armor** you wrapped yourself in when you were fat. Look people in the eye; let yourself be vulnerable and open to new experiences, new people, new ideas.

• **Assert yourself!** Sit in the front row; force yourself to go places and to speak up. There's no reason to hide now.

• **Think positively about yourself.** Keep in mind the fact that the good relationships you're building with your family and your friends come not only from good feelings about them, but also from the good feelings you have about yourself, your new self-confidence and self-esteem.

• **Help make old friends comfortable with you,** if it seems necessary. Some people may not know how to react to a changed you, and your matter-of-fact acceptance of a different situation will put them at ease.

• **Don't accept guilt for things you can't help;** this could send you slipping back into your old eating-for-solace ways. Do what you can to make things right if you're really in the wrong— and then forget the hair shirt.

I'm worth it!

18 Principles Of Successful Dieting

1. Make a Commitment
If achieving your weight goal is important to you, it's worth working for. Even on days when your will power has hoisted the white flag of surrender . . . you can't give up. Successful dieters try to pull themselves out of tailspins that would cause less serious dieters to quit. If you keep bouncing back, you're bound to succeed.

2. Love Yourself
The best reason to diet is because you love yourself and want to look and feel better. Since dieting involves discipline in the areas of eating and exercise, make sure to avoid a self-indulgent orgy of denial by doing plenty of pleasurable "non-food" activities that will help you feel good about yourself. Remember that someone you know loves you a lot.

3. Picture Yourself Thin
Close your eyes, relax and visualize yourself on a scale, weighing in at your target weight. Notice how good it feels to fit into clothes you want to wear and to look slim and healthy. If you can visualize this scene once or twice a day, you'll soon begin to believe that it can be true—and you'll find yourself acting in ways that make it come true.

4. Choose a Diet You Can Live With
The fastest way to bomb out on a diet is to choose one that is so distasteful to you that you can't imagine sticking to it for long. To succeed, you've got to find a diet you really believe in. And that diet has to provide balanced nutrition that will enable you to keep going over the long haul—without making you anemic, dulling your sex drive, turning you into a grouch or giving you other harmful side effects.

5. Get On a Winning Team
Ask your family and friends for help and understanding. Diet with a buddy. Join a support group. Call on your "higher power." The more help you have, the better your odds for success.

6. Be the "Boss" of What Goes Into Your Mouth
If you don't open your mouth and put food into it, you won't eat. If you eat too much, it's not the "fault" of the cook, your hostess or the waiter. Blaming others is a way of avoiding responsibility for your eating.

7. Know Your Weaknesses

Admit you have weaknesses. What are the foods you can't resist? When do you lose control? What situations defeat your diet? Keeping an eating record will tell you where, when, why and how you get into trouble. Then you can successfully make your plans to avoid the problems or be prepared when they arise.

8. Build Up Your Self-Control

Start looking for temptations you know you CAN overcome. Leave something on your plate at the next meal. Pass up bread at dinner or cookies at your coffee break. Take pleasure in these triumphs because they strengthen your will power. Soon you'll be able to refuse dessert even though everyone else at the table is groaning with pleasure.

9. Lose Weight by Burning More Calories Than You Eat

Inactivity is a frequently unrecognized cause of obesity. Many active people can eat more calories than sedentary people and weigh a lot less. It's pretty hard to overeat while you're running, swimming, biking or walking—who wants to lug that extra weight around? Exercise is one of the strongest tools in your dieting kit.

10. Learn New Ways to Shop and Eat

The more you learn about food and nutrition, the easier it is to adopt better shopping and eating habits. You can't binge on sugary, salty or fatty "junk food" you left on the grocery shelf. And you're less likely to overeat broiled fish or chicken than fat-filled hamburgers or ribs. Many dieters achieve long-term weight loss when they learn how to prepare and enjoy more wholesome, nutritious foods.

11. Save Calories by Substituting

Little substitutions mean a lot. Baked potatoes with chives but no sour cream, tuna-fish sandwiches without gobs of mayonnaise, diet soft drinks instead of the sugary kind, broiled chicken instead of fried. It isn't hard to find 100 calories a day to cut by simply switching from something extravagant to a calorie-saving alternative. And 100 calories a day adds up to about 15 extra pounds around your middle in 12 months. If you know your way around the calorie charts, you'll be able to use your brains to beat the bulge. And if you're up on low-calorie seasoning tricks, you may even enjoy the difference.

12. Write Your Own Rule Book

Successful dieters have rules for when, where, how and what to eat—and what to do if they slip up. These rules can help you to resist temptation. Write your rules down and keep them where you can see them every day. You won't feel so terrible if, after eating an "illegal" ice-cream sundae, you go for a brisk half-hour walk or take some other action specified by your own diet rule book.

13. Remember: Out of Sight, Out of Mind

No one's will power is perfect. Keep tempting snacks and treats off kitchen counters, out of see-through canisters and out of the front row in pantries and refrigerators. And choose your position at parties and restaurants so you don't have to look continually at irresistible hors d'oeuvres or desserts.

14. Weigh In Regularly

Your scale will tell you how you're doing on your diet—if you consult it. Successful dieters want lots of feedback—as a token reward for when they're making progress and as a warning for when they're backsliding. You may not consult your scale regularly because you're afraid of receiving "bad news." But if you don't weigh in today and identify the problem, the news could be much worse tomorrow.

15. Listen to Your Stomach

Learn how to tell the difference between a genuine "I'm hungry" message from your stomach and a phony "Feed me" message you get when you see, smell or hear about food. Your stomach may feel satisfied, but if your eyes, nose and ears are "hungry," what do you do? Listen to your stomach.

16. Say "No, Thank You!"

These three words work wonders. Most people who serve you food genuinely want to please you. If you tell them you're not hungry because you filled up on that terrific salad, you give them praise and save your diet without hurting any feelings.

17. Don't Mix Drinking and Dieting

Let's face it: alcohol lowers inhibitions and muddles judgment. Drinking when there's food around can be like lighting a match near a gas tank. If you think it's a problem for you, why take the risk?

18. Start All Over Again Tomorrow

Your burden is lighter when you diet one day at a time. All dieters slip up. Tomorrow you can start over with an absolutely clean slate!

USEFUL
RESOURCES

A Diet for Living
by Jean Mayer (David McKay
Company, 1975).

Act Thin, Stay Thin
by Richard B. Stuart
(W.W. Norton, 1978).

Aerobics
by Kenneth H. Cooper (Bantam,
1972).

*The Barbara Kraus 1980 Calorie
    Guide to Brand Names and
    Basic Foods*
by Barbara Kraus (New American Library, 1979).

Born to Be Slim
by Frank J. Bruno (Harper &
Row, 1978).

Break Out of Your Fat Cell
by Jeane Eddy Westin
(CompCare, 1979).

The Complete Book of Running
by James F. Fixx (Random
House, 1977).

Craig Claiborne's Gourmet Diet
by Craig Claiborne with Pierre
Franey (Times Books, 1981).

Diet by Charles Wetherall
(Wetherall, 1981).

Diets '80: Rating the Diets
by Theodore Berland (Consumer
Guide, 1980).

*Eating is Okay: A Radical
    Approach to Weight Loss*
by Henry A. Jordan, Leonard S.
Levitz and Gordon M. Kimbrell
(New American Library, 1978).

Executive Fitness Newsletter
(Rodale Press, 33 E. Minor St.,
Emmaus, Penn. 18049).

The Family Doctor's Health Tips
by Keith Sehnert, M.D.
(Meadowbrook Press, 1981).

*Fat and Thin: A Natural History
    of Obesity*
by Anne Scott Beller (McGraw
Hill, 1978).

*How to Weigh Less for the Rest
    of Your Life*
by Larry Adcock (Warner Books,
1980).

I'll Never Be Fat Again
by Carole Livingston (Lyle
Stuart, 1980).

Jane Brody's Nutrition Book
by Jane Brody (W. W. Norton,
1981).

The Last Best Diet Book
by Joyce A. Bockar (Stein and
Day, 1980).

Never-Say-Diet Book
by Richard Simmons (Warner
Books, 1980).

The 100 Calorie Book
by Lawrence Sloan and Charles
Gates (Price/Stern/Sloan, 1981).

*Pritikin Program for Diet and
    Exercise*
by Nathan Pritikin with Patrick
M. McGrady, Jr. (Bantam Books,
1979).

*The Taming of the C.A.N.D.Y.
    Monster*
by Vicki Lansky (Meadowbrook
Press, 1978).

Take It Off with Frank
by Frank Field (William Morrow,
1977).

*Weight Watchers New Program
    Cookbook*
by Jean Nidetch (New American
Library, 1978).

Winning the Diet Wars
by Meridee Merzer (Harcourt
Brace Jovanovich, 1980).

*The Woman Doctor's Diet for
    Women*
by Barbara Edelstein (Ballantine
Books, 1977).

INDEX

A

Alcoholic drinks
  see Beverages
Authorities' tips
  Bockar, Dr. Joyce A., 94
  Brody, Jane, 9
  Bruno, Dr. Frank J., 10
  Edelstein, Dr. Barbara, 7, 29, 52
  Field, Dr. Frank, 96
  Fixx, James, 25
  Mayer, Dr. Jean, 19, 24
  Merzer, Meridee, 18
  Stuart, Dr. Richard B., 36
  Wetherall, Charles, 17, 87

B

Backsliding, 95-96
Basic four food groups, 36
Beans, grains and nuts, 38
Beverages, 57, 59, 69, 74, 75, 78, 79, 87-88, 90, 110
Bingeing, 92-94
  Controlling it, 93
Bread
  see Grains
Breakfast, 35, 64, 71
Breathing, 25
Brown-bagging, 64

C

Calorie comparison tables, 37-41, 48
  Selected beans, grains and nuts, 38
  Selected dressings and sauce ingredients, 48
  Selected fruits and vegetables, 40-41
  Selected milk products, 41
  Selected poultry, fish, egg and meat products, 39
Calories, 12, 22, 27, 37-41, 44-45, 63, 79, 109
  see also Exercise
Calories in selected alcoholic drinks, 79
Calories in selected fast foods, 63
Calories in selected soft drinks, 79
Cartoons, 9, 13, 26, 31, 45, 60, 65, 70, 77, 93

Celebrities' tips
  Allen, Jayne Meadows, 76
  Allen, Steve, 50
  Brenner, David, 74
  Diller, Phyllis, 35
  Hill, Sandy, 62
  Hunter, Kim, 24
  Ingels, Marty, 11
Coffee breaks, 66
Convenience foods, 43
Cooking, 46-53

D

Desserts, 49, 57
Diet, selecting a, 8
Dieting
  Alone, 11
  In a group, 9, 10, 91, 103, 108
Dips for vegetables, 88

E

Eating
  Alone, 58
  At friends' homes, 67
  At home, 56-58
  Habits, 7, 28, 56, 58, 64, 109
  Out, 59-61, 62
Eggs, 36, 39
Emotions, 5
  see also Psychological tips
Energy, keeping up, 24
Equipment, 16, 17, 56
Exercise, 22-27, 69, 72, 74, 90, 109
Exercise and eating record, 30

F

Family and friends, 91, 104, 105
  Dieting with, 10
  Establishing new relationships with, 105
  Preventing obesity in, 53
  Support from, 7, 20, 84
Family dinners, 57
Family pressures, 84
Fast foods, 62, 63
Fats, 44, 45, 47, 50
Fish, 36, 39

Free Stuff!

Free Stuff For Parents

Over 250 of the best free and up-to-a-dollar booklets and samples parents can get by mail: • *sample leather, baby spoon, safety latch and drinking cup* • *booklets on pregnancy, childbirth, child care, nutrition, health safety, first aid, reading, day care* • *sample copies of parenting newsletters and magazines and mail order catalogs.* **Only $3.75 ppd.**

Free Stuff For Kids

Over 250 of the best free and up-to-a-dollar things kids can get by mail: • *badges & buttons* • *games, kits & puzzles* • *coins, bills & stamps* • *bumper stickers & decals* • *coloring & comic books* • *posters & maps* • *seeds & rocks.* FREE STUFF FOR KIDS is America's #1 best-selling book for children! **Only $3.75 ppd.**

Free Stuff For Cooks

Over 250 of the best free and up-to-a-dollar booklets and samples cooks can get by mail: • *cookbooks with more than 3,700 recipes for cooking with almonds, fish, wine, eggs, in microwave ovens, clay pots and more* • *money-saving shopping guides and nutrition information* • *sample popcorn ball maker, herb seeds, spices* • *sample food and couponing newsletters.* **Only $3.75 ppd.**

Free Stuff For Home & Garden

Over 350 of the best free and up-to-a-dollar booklets, catalogs and products the home handyman and gardener can get by mail: • *free plans for a new home or addition* • *22 ways to save energy heating and cooling a home* • *furniture-by-mail* • *sample seeds and plants* • *tips on landscaping and vegetable gardening* • *weatherproofing, insulating, and painting guides.* **Only $3.75 ppd.**

Free Stuff For Travelers

Over 1000 free and up-to-a-dollar things travelers can get by mail: • *camping information* • *colorful travel posters* • *festivals and free attractions* • *canoe trips and cruises* • *hotel and motel directories* • *state and national park information* • *beaches and resorts* • *skiing and sailing vacations* • *travel and safety tips* • *maps and guidebooks for thousands of destinations!* **Only $3.75 ppd.**

Meadowbrook's Tips

Family Doctor's Health Tips
by Keith Sehnert, M.D.

Finally, a complete health guide you can really use to take care of yourself! The art of staying in top-notch condition and stopping an illness before it stops you. Dr. Keith Sehnert tells how to adopt a healthier lifestyle; when to call a doctor and how to get the most for your health-care dollar. • *self-diagnois and self-care* • *what to do before you call the doctor* • *fitness, nutrition and mental wellness programs* • *drug side effects* • *recognizing stress and removing it from your life.* **$5.75 ppd.**

Dress Better For Less
by Vicki Audette

When, where and how to find bargains on new and used clothing for men, women and children. Get the clothes you really want—for much less than you ever thought possible! • *finding blue chip clothes in schlock shops* • *strategic shopping tips for finding bargains in 20 different kinds of retail outlets* • *directory of national bargain chains* • *shrewd tips for updating and repairing clothes* • *scouting designer fashions at discount houses.* **Only $5.75 ppd.**

Best Practical Parenting Tips
by Vicki Lansky

Over 1,000 parent-tested ideas for baby and child care that you won't find in Dr. Spock's books. Vicki's newest bestseller is the most helpful collection of new, down-to-earth ideas from new parents ever published. Practical ideas for saving time, trouble and money on such topics as: • *new baby care* • *car travel* • *toilet training* • *dressing kids for less* • *discipline* • *self-esteem.* **Only $5.75 ppd.**

The Best European Travel Tips
by John Whitman

Here's what the other travel guides don't tell about Europe. Whitman's indispensable, easy-to-read tips tell how to avoid tourist traps, rip offs and snafus ... and how to: • *avoid getting ripped-off on currency exchanges* • *get low-cost airfares, tours, hotel rates* • *get your travel documents quickly* • *get through customs quickly* • *how to beat no-vacancy at a hotel* • *how to keep your fanny from being pinched in Italy.* **Only $5.75 ppd.**

Free Things To Do And See

The Best Free Attractions South

From North Carolina to Texas, it's a land swarming with surprises – and over 1,500 of them free:

- *alligator and turtle stalking*
- *cow chip tosses & mule races*
- *free watermelon, bluegrass & barbeque!*

$4.75 ppd.

The Best Free Attractions West

"Just passin' through" from California to Montana? Here's over 1,500 free and exciting attractions for the asking:

- *belching volcanoes & miniature forests*
- *gold panning & quarter horse racing*
- *vineyard tours with free wine samples*

$4.75 ppd.

The Best Free Attractions Midwest

From Kentucky to North Dakota, the Midwest is chock-full of free things:

- *camel rides and shark feedings*
- *stagecoaches and magic tricks*
- *hobo conventions – and free Mulligan stew!*

$4.75 ppd.

The Best Free Attractions East

Over 1,500 irresistible attractions – all free – from West Virginia to Maine:

- *a witchtrial courthouse – with evidence*
- *aviaries where you are caged*
- *the "gentle giants" – and free beer!*

$4.75 ppd.

Order Form

BOOKS (Prices include postage and handling.)

_____ BEST EUROPEAN TRAVEL TIPS . . . . $5.75 ppd.
_____ BEST FREE ATTRACTIONS (EAST) . . . . $4.75 ppd.
_____ BEST FREE ATTRACTIONS (MIDWEST) . . . . $4.75 ppd.
_____ BEST FREE ATTRACTIONS (SOUTH) . . . . $4.75 ppd.
_____ BEST FREE ATTRACTIONS (WEST) . . . . $4.75 ppd.
_____ DRESS BETTER FOR LESS . . . . $5.75 ppd.
_____ FAMILY DOCTOR'S HEALTH TIPS . . . . $5.75 ppd.
_____ FREE STUFF FOR COOKS . . . . $3.75 ppd.
_____ FREE STUFF FOR HOME & GARDEN . . . . $3.75 ppd.
_____ FREE STUFF FOR KIDS . . . . $3.75 ppd.
_____ FREE STUFF FOR PARENTS . . . . $3.75 ppd.
_____ FREE STUFF FOR TRAVELERS . . . . $3.75 ppd.
_____ BEST PRACTICAL PARENTING TIPS . . . . $5.75 ppd.

Name: _____

Address: _____

_____ Zip _____

In ordering more than
6 books, please write
to us for quantity dis-
count rates.

$ Total enclosed _____
Make checks payable to:
Meadowbrook Press, Dept. **SDT-DM**
I bought my book at ☐ my bookclub ☐ bookstore ☐ other retail store